CATAPULTS

- and -

KINGFISHERS

Teaching Poetry in Primary Schools

·PIE CORBETT·
·BRIAN MOSES·

Oxford University Press · 1986

Oxford University Press, Walton Street, Oxford OX2 6DP

Oxford London
New York Toronto Melbourne Auckland
Petaling Jaya Singapore Hong Kong Tokyo
Delhi Bombay Calcutta Madras Karachi
Nairobi Dar es Salaam Cape Town

and associated companies in
Beirut Berlin Ibadan Nicosia

Oxford is a trade mark of Oxford University Press

Moses, Brian
  Catapults and kingfishers: teaching poetry
  in primary schools.
  1. English literature—Study and teaching
  (Elementary)—Great Britain 2. Poetry—
  Study and teaching (Elementary)—Great Britain
  I. Title II. Corbett, Peter John
  372.6'4 LB1575.5.G7

  ISBN 0-19-919069-0

Phototypeset by Tradespools Ltd., Frome

Printed and bound in Great Britain by
Hazell Watson & Viney Limited,
Member of the BPCC Group,
Aylesbury, Bucks

CONTENTS

ABOUT THE AUTHORS

Pie Corbett is Headmaster of Lynsted C.P. School in Kent. Brian Moses is Senior Master and Language Consultant at Freda Gardham C.P. School in Rye, East Sussex.

The authors both lecture and run workshop sessions on teaching poetry. They are poets themselves, taking part in the Poetry Society's 'Poets in Schools' scheme and in South East Arts' 'Writers in Schools' programme. Pie Corbett was also writer in residence attached to the Kent Literature Festival in 1985. Brian Moses was co-editor of the S.E. Arts anthology *Identity Parade* – featuring poetry and prose by young people in Kent, Surrey and East Sussex.

Children from schools where Pie Corbett and Brian Moses have taught have been successful in both local and national competitions for young writers on several occasions including those run by W.H. Smith and the Poetry Society of Great Britain. Some of the winning poems have been featured on both ITV and BBC television.

Children spend much of their time talking, laughing and joking – in fact, many of them have so much to say that it is surprising that when they come to write, often they cannot think of even the first few words. Indeed, the most talkative children may well be the ones who find it the hardest to write anything down. Often the quick-witted 'joker' of the class is the one who struggles painfully over every word. Why should this be, and more important how can we channel this flow of words and inventive ability into writing?

Quite simply, children fail to write well because they are afraid of 'getting it wrong' and because they have not been taught writing as a skill. Many of us realise that if children are given sheets of sugar paper, paints, paintbrushes and allowed to 'get on with it', not much will happen – they need to be taught certain skills; how to hold the brush, mix paints, observe an object, explore shape, line, texture, colour, use perspective.... They need to be shown how to use techniques and be given a variety of stimuli to practise such skills. Writing can also be taught. There are techniques to be learnt, and certain writing ideas can be used to practise these.

Many children do not like writing because it becomes a dull task that has nothing to do with their own thoughts, feelings and opinions. It is little fun and often does not challenge their inventive nature. The ideas in this book have all been tried and tested in many classrooms. They are easy to use, enjoyed by children, and can be used to develop writing skills and techniques.

● COLLAGE POEMS

This book uses 2 different approaches. Firstly, there are 'list' or 'collage' poems. Each line starts with the same phrase and all the child has to do is tack on a new idea each time.

> *I like the taste of ... sweet strawberries.*
> *I like the taste of ... sizzling, salty bacon.*

This approach is particularly successful with children who have little confidence in their writing ability unless they have a structure on which to hang their thoughts. Many of the ideas are a chance to invent a joke or involve a surreal twist which appeals to children's sense of fun.

> *He was so unlucky*
> *that his butter melted in the fridge.*

> *He was so unlucky*
> *that he lost his lucky charm.*

It is this element of inventing a joke that so often wins over a reluctant writer.

> *When I blow my own trumpet*
> *my dolls run to the next room for shelter.*
> *When I blow my own trumpet*
> *pictures fall off the wall*
> *and the next door neighbours start packing.*
> *When I blow my own trumpet*
> *people sigh and turn their backs on me*
> *and the crack in the wall grows bigger.*

This 'surreal' approach to playing with words stretches children's minds to create new ways of expressing ideas that offer a real challenge. The subject matter is endless.

> *My words are made of matches*
> *I'll strike you alight with them.*
> *My words are made of stones*
> *I'll catapult them across the room.*

The only pitfall with this approach is that sometimes the children's lines will be too brief and boring.

> *I like the sound of dogs.*
> *I like the sound of a car.*

Stop the child before the list becomes too long and ask him or her to add to each idea – "What kind of dog, what is he doing, where is he?"

> *I like the sound of my angry wolfhound*
> *leaping over the fence in the park.*

"What colour is the car, where is it travelling to, what noise is it making, what does it look like?"

> *I like the sound of the red sports car*
> *as it zooms down the road to London*
> *like a kingfisher.*

The ideas for list poems start quite simply and become quite complex for older children, perhaps even involving a syllable pattern.

> *What do stones dream of?*
> *Moss clinging to their cool skins.*
> *What do bones dream of?*
> *Blood pulsing by their blunt buds.*

The secret of a good collage poem is that each idea should be entirely different and new. Once children become used to this approach they will invent their own list poems.

- *I close my eyes and I see*
a dark shape crawling around my head.

  I close my eyes and I see
tiny fragments of colours
wriggling about like insects.

  I close my eyes and I see
muddy faces staring hard at me.

  I close my eyes and I see
darkness is dead.

  I close my eyes and I see
black demons swirling like smoke.

  I open my eyes and I see
the beautiful world around me.

  Deborah, 8 yrs.

● WHY DOES IT WORK?

When children are writing, two things are going on – firstly they are trying to make up the piece of writing, then they are coping with the problems of getting the words onto paper. For many young children the problems of getting the right spelling, punctuation and neat handwriting are uppermost in their minds. By giving them a repeating structure one of the 'worries' is taken away from them. Furthermore, if you tell the class not to worry about spelling at this stage, but simply to get their ideas down on paper, then they are free to concentrate on selecting good ideas and vivid words to work with. Once their ideas are written down they can then concentrate on writing them up neatly and accurately. This is why 'remedial' children and reluctant writers often find a new confidence with this approach – the ideas appeal, the normal constraints are lifted and the job has been divided into two sections.

● USING A MODEL

An extension of using a collage poem is to use, as a stimulus, a poem by an established writer. Often you will find that children will want to use some of the ideas, words or forms of the original. This should not be seen as a weakness but part of their development as they try their hand at something new. Discussion, word collecting and the child's own experience will bring the feel of the individual to the writing. Using other poems as models plays an important part in helping children

7

to develop a style of their own. From each lesson they may bring something new to their writing experience that later surfaces as an echo in their own style. Compare the following two examples by Kathryn, a third year junior, set alongside the stimulus poems for each lesson.

Heron

A gawky stilt-
ed fossicker a-
mong reeds, the
gun-grey-green
one, gauntly
watchful cold-
eye, stiff on
single column,a
brooding hump
of wind-ruffled
feather-brain
feathering the
blue shall-
ows,with one
scaly claw
poised drip-
ping –

     wades
the pebbled lake,
prints the mudflat,
scorns the noi-
sy fancy oy-
stercatchers' talk,
stalks, tall, to
his flat ramshack-
le nest,or shack
of slack sticks,
with three dull
greeny eggs
by a bul-
rush grove –

till the snaky neck
coils back
and strikes, beak
darts and spears
quick fish,
fish, fish
silvery-rich
fisher-king dish,

Hyena

I am waiting for you.
I have been travelling all morning through the bush and not eaten.
I am lying at the edge of the bush
on a dusty path that leads from the burnt-out kraal.
I am panting, it is midday, I found no water-hole
I am very fierce without food and although my eyes are screwed to slits against the sun you must believe that I am ready to spring.

What do you think of me?
I have a rough coat like Africa.
I am crafty with dark spots
like the bush-tufted plains of Africa.
I sprawl as a shaggy bundle of gathered energy like Africa sprawling in its waters.
I trot, I lope, I slaver, I am a ranger.
I hunch my shoulders. I eat the dead.

Do you like my song?
When the moon pours hard and cold on the veldt
I sing, and I am the slave of darkness.
Over the stone walls and the mud walls and the ruined places and the owls, the moonlight falls.
I sniff a broken drum. I bristle. My pelt is silver.
I howl my song to the moon – up it goes.
Would you meet me there in the waste places?

It is said I am a good match
for a dead lion. I put my muzzle
at his golden flanks, and tear. He
is my golden supper, but my tastes are easy.
I have a crowd of fangs, and I use them.
Oh and my tongue – do you like me
when it comes lolling out over my jaw
very long, and I am laughing?
I am not laughing.

and then in the lone-
ly white lazy
hazy afternoon
he rises slowly
in a big zig-
zag heavy over
sultry fens
and windmill vanes,
flapping silently
in the land of wings.

Edwin Morgan

The Heron

Cold,
watchful face,
Standing still,
Thin, spindly leg.
Planted in
the crystal shallows,
A humped
watcher.
Cruel
eyes peering at
the world,
A sharp skinny
beak
A ruffled bundle,
of grey feathers
A thin neck doubled
back
Ready to spear a
fish
Splish, splash,
Silverdash,
fisherking
fish-snatch
A gleaming morsel,
hangs
motionless
It stalks to the nest
A shack of sticks
It zig zags
into the hazy
white distance
A flapping
Ruffled shape
far away in the sky.

But I am not snarling either, only
panting in the sun, showing you
what I grip
carrion with.

I am waiting
for the foot to slide,
for the heart to seize,
for the leaping sinews to go slack,
for the fight to the death to be fought to the
death, for a glazing eye and the rumour of blood.
I am crouching in my dry shadows
till you are ready for me.
My place is to pick you clean
and leave your bones to the wind.

Edwin Morgan

Tiger

Watching, waiting, crouching low,
For you to walk in to my trap
My sleek pink tongue,
Hangs out of my jaw,
As I pant in the heat
of the scorching sun.
I am striped like a humbug.
My feet are padded,
Like a cushion, as I lie
Waiting for you,
I close my eyes to slits
As the suns scorching beams
beat down on my back.
But when night falls
The moon rises
Its rays are cold
It cools me down from the burning sun
So I sit on a rock and sing my song
I am waiting for you
When you come,
I will pounce on you,
Dig my claws in and tear
at the flesh,
I will eat every bit of you,
After I will leave your bones
Picked clean by my fangs
To bleach in the sun.

Kathryn Hoblin, 8 yrs.

9

We can see how she captures the line length, rhythm and rough structure of each poem. She borrows certain words and uses them effectively. She also brings her own additions to the poems. In *The Heron* she uses Edwin Morgan's rhythmic play on words which emphasises the speed that a heron uses to snatch a fish –

> *. . . and spears*
> *quick fish,*
> *fish, fish,*
> *silvery-rich*
> *fisher-king dish . . .*

to great effect herself –

> *. . . Ready to spear a*
> *fish,*
> *Splish,*
> *Splash,*
> *Silverdash,*
> *fisherking,*
> *fish-snatch . . .*

The accidental, internal rhyme, where she describes the Heron standing in the shallows, combined with the layout of the words creates a crisp, effective image.

> *Standing still.*
> **Thin**
> **Spin***dly leg,*
> *Planted in*
> *the crystal*
> *shallows,*

The echo of sounds in 'crystal' and 'cruel', 'neck', 'back' and 'beak', 'stalks' and 'sticks' create a connecting rhythm that is her own.

In The *Hyena* she writes about a *Tiger*, adding her own more homely imagery –

> *I am striped like a humbug.*
> *My feet are padded*
> *like cushions.*

Later stories and poems by Kathryn showed that her ability to make other people's writings her own had been a point of growth. The instructions for the following poem were to choose an object or feeling and to write six brief observations. Each idea had to contain an unusual twist of language or startling image, (see also *Swimming* on page 69, which was written quite alone with no discussion or stimulus).

Six ways of looking at a pond

1 A pond's ripple shatters faces into misery and lines.
2 A pond reflects the memories of children playing by its edge.
3 Sheets and sheets of lace gently laid on top of each other glistening in the sunlight.
4 A pond is a net of faces and fish being dragged behind a trawler.
5 A pond is a glittering pocket of beads trickling into a bag.
6 A pond is a swan's paradise, where she gazes into the darkness.

Kathryn Hoblin, 8yrs.

Children will often reuse words, images, ideas and forms that have been tried before. It was not surprising when I read Steven's poem about dreams to recall that we had written about hands a few weeks previously. He began –

● **Dreams**

*An iron bar might dream of melting
then drying, to take the form of a
butterfly.
A window sill might dream of egg
being cracked on it, the liquid
setting into glass.
The sun might dream of turning into
the moon on your thumbnail.*

● **OPEN POEMS**

The second approach allows the child to choose his or her own pattern and write without the use of a repetitive phrase. Some children will want to write prose, others will want to try to form a pattern of words upon the page. The only rule to forming 'word patterns' is that the reader must be able to read it.

So:

```
                    fox        through
        sly                    the        creeps
                stealthily
        wood        the
```

becomes: *The sly fox*
                                      creeps
                            stealthily
                            through the wood.

Children can be asked to 'make a pattern on the page with the words'. A good way to show them how this can be done is by selecting a variety of different shaped poems for handwriting practice – or by doing a class poem on the board. Really it does not matter whether the piece of writing is written as prose or in a pattern – as long as it is well written. There seems little point in chopping up good prose to try to turn it into a poem.

● **SHOULD IT RHYME?**

Many children will attempt to use rhyme. Generally this ends in disaster and there is often good reason to ban the use of rhyme initially, until the class has developed its use of language considerably. At first the child's attention may be focused entirely upon rhyming the last word in the second line with the last word in the first line.

So, when a child writes –

The sly fox crept through the wood

the next line has to be twisted to end with 'could, good, hood, would, or should'. This leads to dishonesty that at its worst becomes gibberish.

●   ***There was a cat called Tony.***
He was spikey and looked like a pony.
He lives in a tree
and he drinks cups of tea.
Every morning when he goes to work
he meets a friend called Peark.
He chews rats,
varieties of bats.
He has a drink at bed
When all is done and said.

Compare the above poem by Stuart, 8 years old, with the following –

●   **Cats**

Snowy creeps gingerly down the alley. His eyes glow. His claws bend. He sights a figure. His back arches like a bridge. He pounces on the figure, rips and tears. His teeth are as sharp as an axe. His tongue is as rough as rocks.

Without the limitations of a rhyming scheme Kevin (9 years old) has written a short piece that is more honest and direct than Stuart's. (Kevin was a boy who had been classed as 'remedial').

Rhythm and rhyme should not become a forced exercise. As children increase their facility to use words, develop their vocabulary and increase the speed and flow with which they write, a natural rhythm and occasional rhymes begin to develop. Before we think of rhymes, however, there are other skills that are more important to learn.

If we presented you with a pile of wood, hammer, saw, plane, nails and workbench, could you make a Welsh dresser? The answer is almost certainly no. You would have to learn how to cut wood to a certain length, how to plane accurately, how to make joints... Indeed, it would take several years of apprenticeship before you could attempt the finished article. The same applies to writing a poem – before you can consider using rhymes or metrical patterns. There are other much more basic skills to grasp – first there is the ability to observe, and the next is the ability to select the right word, to be a 'word-searcher'.

●   **A TYPICAL LESSON**

Let us imagine a typical lesson, using the *'open'* method of writing. It will start with a stimuli:

a   *An object* – *a stone, a wooden box, a tree ...*
b   *An event* – *snowfall, school fête, swimming ...*
c   *A photo* – *old people, stormy sea, dancers ...*
d   *A poster* – *volcano, surreal painting ...*
e   *Music* – *'Pictures from an exhibition' ...*
f   *An animal* – *guinea pig, dog, lamb, parrot ...*
g   *A recalled, shared or common experience* – *night in my room, being alone, having a bath, running away.*

●   **THE STIMULI**

Most of us glide through life unaware of what is going on around us. One day a class of 3rd year juniors were asked what colour the side of the class hut was. Only two children could remember. When we present children with a stimulus to write about we must train them first to OBSERVE closely. With infants this may mean bringing their gaze back to the object, with juniors it may mean probing them to use all their senses to react. We encourage our class to study a stimulus in detail, we train them to observe by questioning them, drawing their attention to the details – "What colours can you see, what does the shape remind you of, how old is it, whose was it, what is it like when the sun shines on it, what word describes how it moves?". In this way we constantly focus their attention in a meditative manner.

● THE DISCUSSION

Poems are made out of words. Whoever it was that said "count the words and the poems will look after themselves" was on the right track – especially for our purposes – to produce clear, honest, vivid descriptions. Having observed, we must then decide on which words to use to describe what we have experienced. When you or I sit down to write we search around in our minds to try and find the right words – often several words present themselves and we select the one we feel most appropriate. Young children don't do this in the same way. They tend to write down the first word that comes into their heads without any reflection on whether the words selected are suitable or not. The following piece of writing, by a secondary school girl, is the product of an education that has failed to develop her vocabulary and left her unaware of the possibilities of choosing different words to illustrate her writing.

●   Sharks

There are big ones Great ones and small ones.
And there are blue ones white and grey ones to.
And there are jawes to their big sharp white teeth.
I am afraid of there big mouthes opening and closing them.
Also there is a big tiger shark.

What we have to do is to train our children to become 'wordsearchers', to actually show them how we filter words through our minds and select the most suitable one. So, we begin by prompting the children to offer us words to describe an experience, and we collect these words on the blackboard. By questioning carefully we can guide children to the detail of the experience, and to use their five senses and respond with a variety of words and images. Initially this may be difficult because the children will be thinking on a 'surface level'.

I often think of the mind as having two vocabulary levels. On the surface are the words we use in everyday conversation and these are the words that the children will initially offer.

14

They are perhaps useful in conversation but do not contain the rich variety of language that illuminates an experience for the writer and reader. To describe snow, words such as 'wet', 'white', 'soft' and 'cold' will spring to their minds first of all. The deeper level of vocabulary contains all the words we know the meaning of but do not often use in conversation. The majority of the children will recognise them but just haven't thought of them. By questioning them you prompt them to dig deeper into their minds for these words – bitter, bleak, bare, barren, brittle, fragile, frail, delicate, lace, swirl, whirl, twirl, curl, gleam, glisten, glitter, scuff, crunch, scrunch, tread, imprint etc. . . . This part of the lesson is the most important. The quality of the words you collect reflects in the quality of what the children write. You are showing them how to 'wordsearch', build vocabulary and observe. By the end of the year they may well not need this support. Indeed, the ultimate aim is to reduce this part of the lesson and channel the discussion to a deeper level, considering ideas and methods of presentation. But initially it is vital for the teacher to do this groundwork.

The idea of a 'word list' went out of favour some years ago. The difference here is that the list is made up of the children's words and that they can use as many or as few of the words as they wish, often adding more of their own. The list gives support to poorer writers, it helps as a spelling aid so that concentration is not broken by searching in a dictionary, and when children are stuck with their poem and need a new idea they can glance at the board, where a word may send them off in a new direction. Most importantly, you are teaching them how to select and value words.

●   **GETTING THEM WRITING**

Now the board is crammed with words, ideas have been flying round the room for 20 minutes. It is time to write. **1** We write quickly – I often set a limit of 15 minutes as this produces a sense of urgency and often an unbroken flow of writing that has a natural rhythm and logical sense to it. There is nothing worse than a piece of writing that has been agonised over by an 8 year old, with a chewed pencil stub, for 50 minutes. **2** We write quietly – no-one can become absorbed in recalling an experience and finding suitable words to describe it if they are talking or have a background of disturbing chatter. **3** When we write we often close our eyes and re-imagine the exerience – "What was it like, hold it in your mind as you write". **4** We have no interruptions for 'spellings' (or any other reason). The important thing is to get the writing done without breaking the flow of thought. All the surface errors can be corrected later. **5** Make sure that the instructions are clear, the children all have paper, sharpened pencils and a rubber. Try to make the change from talking to writing brief, and create a working sense of urgency. Many teachers use scrap paper or a rough book for this stage of writing. One side can be used for the initial attempt and the other for rewriting. Some teachers use poetry folders. **6** Now the teacher can move round encouraging and making suggestions. First of all help those who find it hard to start, perhaps even sitting with them. Suggest several opening lines or avenues of thought, ask the child to tell you about his or her own experiences and use these as a basis for the piece of writing. Secondly, circulate round the room to ensure that everyone is getting on with it.

●   **HOW CHILDREN WRITE**

While children are writing, many thoughts and feelings are buzzing through their heads. Some to do with what to say, some to do with the mechanics of writing and some quite irrelevant....

> *"I'll try to write more than a page this time. What word describes that word best? Which word fits in here? Have I spelt this right? Oh bother! I've forgotten to do a margin. I wonder when break is. My pencil is getting blunt..."*

A lot is going on and if they are to become good at writing they will have to cope with all this, at the same time, successfully. The problem can be helped by working towards a situation where the task is done in two halves – firstly, getting the ideas down on paper and secondly, rewriting them neatly and accurately. This way we end up with the best of both worlds. First they concentrate on finding good ideas and words. Then they concentrate on making sure the spelling is accurate, writing neat, punctuation and grammar sound. This does not mean that their first draft should be untidily written – children should never be encouraged into poor habits. It means that the second draft will be written out with great care.

For young children this notion may prove tedious and spoil the pleasure of writing. It should be introduced to older juniors or when the teacher feels the class are ready. It should not be done on every occasion.

Some older children will make notes before writing and have

several attempts at a poem before settling on a final draft. The following word list was jotted down by a third year girl, Debbie, whilst watching a series of slides on insects.

Spiders

small	spinnerets	translucent	
water	abdomen	strawberry	large
hunter	palps	tiny	untidy
evil	crablike	timid	web
leopard	skinned	transparent	tarantula
green	zebidy	mouldy	
common	knobbly	dark	irregular
spider	tiger	seaweed	deadly untidy
prickles	legs	blotchy	web

on dirty slender twig gigantic
legs old rapid mover
web marrow body bright light
green velvety spider
blue silky abdomen telescope legs
small black spider
fantastic diamond neckless
daddy long legs
succulent strawberry

She then makes her *'first try'*.

●   *(first try)* **Spider**

> *Minute spinnerets*
> *Slender twig legs*
> *(Velt) Velvety brown abdomen*
> *Eight spindly legs.*
> *Dark blotchy body.*
> *Timid but deadly.*
> *A harmless creature.*
> *So evil.*
> *Yet so soft and small.*
> *Long translucent legs.*

She has tried to describe the spider and say something about how it seems so harmless yet in its own way it is a deadly creature. However, she was displeased with this and wanted to try and show the spider 'catching a fly'.

●   *(second try)*

> *Small cold crevice.*
> *The spider waits.*
> *Still as stone*
> *A jerk.*

The silky lines move.
  Like telephone wires.
carrying messages to
the spider.
The spider awakes.
Quick as the flicker
of a fire.
The spider is upon him
A small black
plump spider.
A cold death
The spider sucks the blood
A cold blooded murder.
The spider creeps back.
back to its evil home.

Though she preferred this attempt, in the second half of the poem the action takes over and it begins to read like a 'dramatised' story. In her final draft she keeps her effective images – 'Still as stone', 'The silky lines move/Like telegraph wires/Sending messages' and 'The spider awakes/Quick as the flicker of a flame' – and kills the fly off much more quickly, avoiding repetition of the words 'The spider' too many times. The result is much more crisp, precise –

becomes
> *carrying messages to*
> *the spider*
>
> *Sending messages.*

After all, she does not need to state to whom the messages are being sent.

becomes
> *Quick as the flicker*
> *of a fire*
>
> *Quick as the flicker of a flame.*

The word flame echoes the fl in flicker, which in turn echoes the ck in quick. This added rhythm gives the image more speed and emphasis. The final version reads.

● **Spider**

Small cold crevice
The spider waits
Still as stone
A jerk
The silky lines move
Like telephone wires,

Sending messages
The spider awakes
Quick as the flicker of a flame
The spider is upon him
A cold death
The spider creeps back to its evil home.

● **WHILE THEY WRITE**

The teacher moves round the room, trying not to distract,
"Don't forget what I told you all about...", or be glib, "That's
lovely...". Where a child has established a flow of writing,
don't interrupt. If someone is stuck you might direct them to
someone else's method. "Look at how Jason has set out his
poem". For those who are unsure, give reassurance. "Yes,
this is an effective start, keep going now". Suggest several
new ideas, new lines of thought, choices of words to anyone
faltering. Ask questions to get them to extend their writing,
"What happened next?" "What did you notice about...?"
"What did it remind you of?" Bring their attention back to
words on the board that they haven't used and that might
produce a new direction. Remind them of parts of the
experience that they have not yet written about, "You've not
mentioned...", "What about adding a bit on...?" A useful
method is to suggest that the child writes a sentence or few
words to describe each part of the experience. So, when
writing about a stuffed fox, Hayley describes his eyes, fangs,
body, tail, nose and toe nails with careful precision.

The Fox

The fox
  creeps over
    the
      frost   His bushy
        at night   tail trailing
His ruby red eyes   on
  shining   the white ground
   in   his black nose sniffing
    pitch of darkness   along
     His white fangs   the grass
     sticking   for food.
      out   His
       of his jaws   toe-nails
        his russet body   digging, deeply
         swaying as he walks.   into the ground.

Hayley, 8 yrs.

Initially, with all children we will be offering praise for the well chosen words, and plenty of encouragement. Later, you can also draw the children's attention to the weak points. This is a sensitive area and it is up to the teacher to judge the appropriate moment for each child when encouragement starts to involve a search for ways to make a piece of writing even better. The angle should be, "Can we find a better way of putting this? Can you think of another word?" and never, "This bit is bad". To help children find their weaknesses we have to start by showing where they are and offering help to overcome them.

If a poor start has been made then a totally new beginning may be necessary. "If you're finding it hard to rhyme, leave it and start again in a different way. Look at how Jane has started."

I like to tick the words, images and ideas I like, and put a dotted line under weak parts:

> As the dragon strolls √ by you see its
> scaley √ legs. Its fat √ stomach bulging √ out
> as large as a house. His eyes round like
> grapefruits. √ Steel is his tongue and as dry
> as a
> wall. √ Strong √ claws rushing along the rocks.
> I see him fly. His tail is long like a
> stream. Jaws are big as paper. iron bars.

You can see how I ticked seven words and underlined 'paper' as being a poor image. She changed this to 'iron bars'. This was one of the first pieces of writing that she successfully completed by second draft stage.

Repetitions can often become monotonous and sometimes show a lack of thought in selecting an appropriate word. The end of a poem 'She is' by a 7 year old illustrates this. . . .

> *She is like a **small** gust of wind.*
> *She is like a **great** butterfly flying over a shrub.*
> *She is like a **small** humming bird hovering.*
> *She is like a **great** bird rising to the sun.*
> *She is like a **small** bee buzzing away.*
> *She is like a moon in the sky.*
>
> *Change all those **smalls** and **greats** . . .*

Though at times repetition can be a powerful device for building up an effect. Notice how in the next poem Deborah builds up a rhythmic effect by repeating 'said he'. The inversion distances God, makes him seem more powerful. She also repeats the words 'the bush' 3 times very close together. The repetitions add force to each statement.

● *The burning bush*

The bush blazed, brightly before Moses.
A voice came to him.
Take off your shoes said he.
Who are you? said Moses.
I am the God of this mountain said he.
Take off your shoes for this is Holy ground.
Moses came nearer no more.
He took off his shoes and knelt down before
the bush.
The bush blazed like the white inside of
the sun.
And yet Moses could see that the bush
was unchanged.
Then God spoke one single word.
His name.
And power from God poured into Moses
As wine filling a cup.

Deborah Blanchett, 8 yrs.

Watch out for descriptions that do not tell us enough about the experience.

> *The dog came out and chased me*
> *home. I was afraid.*

Ask the child to add more details to bring the picture alive. Use questions. . . .

> *The black dog snarled. His beady eyes*
> *fixed me like slits of fire. His body*
> *tensed and I knew that he would*
> *leap . . .*

After all, we are not looking for a report of an event but a recreation of the experience, so that when we read it we relive it ourselves. I am often saying to children, "A man chased me home last night. Is that a story – is it exciting? No – to turn it into a story you would need all the details. What sort of night was it? What sort of place was it? What did I hear first? Could I see anything? How did I feel . . . ?"

Do the verbs give drama to the sentences? Do they bring the writing alive? Can you hear and feel them? A recent poem by Bonny started:

> *I got in the bath and my shadow got in and*
> *washed.*

The two 'gots' were changed to 'clambered' and 'slithered'. Later in a story she wrote

> *I saw a small shadow coming towards me.*

She altered that 'coming' to 'sliding'. Glenn wrote recently 'I knew I could go back and get some provisions'. His rewrite used 'swim' and 'fetch'.

Do the adjectives give power to the nouns? Do they make the description form a vivid picture in our minds? Are they precise? If there are too many, choose the most appropriate. In the following piece Richard has started to search for effective adjectives to bring his description of a plant he has just drawn alive – *bright, green, delicate, grey, wide, withered, wrinkled. . . .*

Plant

Plant

A stain of bright green mould
stings your delicate peeling bark.
Lichen surrounds you
as grey moss covers your bulk.
Your wide withered arms
camouflaged by creeping,
introducing leaves which bulge and
are supple as palm trees.
Your weathered growth rings
lie stuck like splodges on the
wrinkled stump. You are
getting old little plant, you can tell –
you have minute whiskers
urging from your branches.
The pattern ingraved on you
repeats like a record carrying
on and on until it smothers you completely.

Richard Cobbold, 10 yrs.

Are the images successful? Do they ring true?

> *'The blood ran out of my arm like a river . . .'*

"Does blood run out of your arm like a river? How does it move? – it dribbles, drips, seeps. Which word would be best?"

It is often best not to be too critical. Give plenty of praise and perhaps gently make one suggestion for an improvement. Nothing will inhibit children more than criticism, or fear of failure. This whole process must be done with the utmost sensitivity for fear of spoiling the children's sense of pleasure in writing.

Finally, is the poem unfolding in a logical, clear manner?

All this is quite a task and it is impossible – perhaps fortunately – to give much attention amongst a large class.

But we are working towards a situation where the children begin to revise their work as they write, and can analyse their own strengths and weaknesses.

How can we encourage such an attitude with a class of 35?

1 As suggested above, the teacher can make suggestions and question individuals while they are writing.

2 The teacher can write a class poem on the board, using the children's ideas, and show how words can be sifted, swopped around, selected, and ideas originated that then spark off another idea; also refining sentences, and putting them into an appropriate order.

3 Read some of the children's work aloud and ask the class to listen for the pieces they liked best. Later on, ask them to also listen for pieces they feel could be made better ... but they have to come up with a helpful suggestion themselves. Several suggestions can be given and then it is left to the writer to choose what to do.

Looking at one child's work

Let us look at a poem that the teacher has 'gone over' with the author. Can you work out the reasoning behind his marking?

●   ***The Tollund man***

He lay bedded in the earth,
(The preserved man) lay dead
and sleeping.
His face is like a bronze
bust.
The (wrinkled) face lays still
in the peat.
A rope dangles in the cool mud
His body is wedged in between
the earth.
He waited sleeping for 2000
years to see the sun.

John Flann, 10 yrs.

1 Don't start with 'He' but 'The preserved man' – it is more direct and means he can avoid repeating 'lay'.

2 To avoid repeating 'face' move 'wrinkled'.

3 Miss out 'is' to make the image more direct, the line shorter, less wordy and more effective.

4 Which is better 'The wrinkled face' or 'His wrinkled face'? Use 'His' as you have already mentioned him.

5 'Dangles' is circled – can a rope dangle in mud when it has been preserved there for 2,000 years? Is 'dangle' suitable?

6 Miss out 'is' and 'in' to turn the line from wordy prose to rhythmic poetry – it 'sounds' better.

7 Should he add a word to describe the earth?

8 Finally, correct the spelling errors and check the punctuation.

This attempt to write a poem about the Tollund man was followed several pages later by a poem triggered off by a photo found in an old album, of 'The Tomb of Lazarus'. This time the writing is more sustained, the poem has more unity. Has he learnt how to tackle successfully a more ambitious project, on his own?

● **The Tomb of Lazarus**

1

Here you lie cold as stone,
Your body is bound in bandages,
The bolder slowly turns to
                    one side
The man of miracles rose you
                    from the dead
You stood in front of Jesus
who unrapped your bandages from
your withered body
You lay in that tomb for four days
sleeping silently
Your soul has called your new
                    life in to you.

2

In this photo we see your
tomb with toothless arabs
smiling
We see a door way with
no door. The photo tells us
what it was like in
the past
But then one boy
found this album
with a dusty cover
and old photos.
The cloth on the
cover is
ripped and old
like the bandages
which Lazarus wore
when he died.

The second part of the poem becomes much more like prose but he ties the poem up neatly at the end. Earlier writing had been more descriptive – for example, this piece recalling a summer holiday in Barbados!

.●
The sea churns
sucks, spits out water
jelly fish quiver
palm trees sway
speckles of tar
rubbish and cans

coke bottles lay
summer houses are silent
Dogs race about
shells tunnel
motionless lizards lay.

By the end of the Christmas term, he has developed a new style of layout and his own 'prose/poetry' voice, using long lines. This 'snow' piece contains the old junior school favourite 'Jack Frost' and some over-use of adjectives, 'gentle, delicate, bitter'. However, his idea of a 'transparent seal' is quite startling.

The snow queen
she wanders through
a cold frost bitten
palace to do a
winter deed.
With her velvet veil
on the frozen grass.
Frozen by a transparent
seal.
Up jumps Jack Frost to paint
the world
with ice.

She makes the palace of
gentle delicate bitter
candy floss
Jack, with his spikey hair
paints the trees
with cold swift
hands
The icicles jab in your
fingers and makes
them bleed.

John Flann, 10yrs.

Early in January he is still using the same style. In this next poem however, he drops into prose and the action takes over 'He gets up and . . .' after a dramatic start with a striking image of loneliness 'Bound to a world . . .'. He has an idea of likening the house to heaven and hell, but cannot sustain it. Finally, it does not work. He ends rather weakly travelling 'in a rocket made out of gold'.

●   **Dark Dawns**

He wanders through
a dark passage
of cold creaking
floor boards
Bound to a world
where no man has
been.
His feet scuffle and

scrape on that dark
dawn morning
His mind is
in a dream
which only a mind
like his can think
of.
He gets up and
turns on the

radio it wakes
him up.
His basement is hell
and his bedroom
is heaven.
The floors were stars
and the sheets were galaxys.
He travelled in a rocket
made out of gold.

Several months later he has moved towards writing his work
as prose. His concerns are more with abstract ideas 'peaceful
thoughts' and 'truthful words'. He tries to liken death to a
rubber band but it does not seem powerful enough as an
image. Again, he ends weakly.

● ### My Grandfather

In peaceful thoughts he lies,
of golden streams, as he chatters
with truthful words,
muttering utter darkness
drowning his thoughts.
In silence of glinting light.
His auburn hair
lies on his coller of golden
thread. He wears a hat with
feathers speckling the brim.
The solem old man lies
contented of life or death
expanding like a rubber band
till it snaps dead.

The final piece is written entirely as prose. It mixes direct
observation with a new interest in playing with rhyming
words, 'night, light', 'muttering, utter'. His opening creates a
strange mood. Does it matter if we cannot fully grasp what he
wants to say? Here he is trying out his language and enjoying
it! We can also hear the influence of Dylan Thomas and
'Under Milk Wood'.

● ### Village

The flame of a night light in a cold descent. Village children
muttering, utter words among the deaf and blind. Houses
blind as bats with chimney pots and sillhouetted crows on the
outline of T.V. aerials: The black boats bobbing on dark
shadowy night sea: A power house with a deafening hum, a
sign saying 'Danger high voltage'. Cats prowl around the
plane trees. The street lights burning on the dusty cobbled

path with ancient dried seaweed tangled in the stones.
Outside my window leaves are suspended on cold frozen
window sill.

He does not try to 'find an ending' and the piece is better for
it. Over the year he has tried several ways of writing and has
settled on a prose style. He has overcome his urge to
conclude and force an image. He is trying a new rhyming
technique internally. He is writing more, and sustaining the
writing to a greater effect. He is now 'trying on' another
author's 'atmosphere'. It is helpful to view children's
development as writers and not just to look at isolated
poems. Encourage them to keep poetry files.

●   **A WORD OF WARNING**

There is a long way to go before children can revise their own
work once it is written. This is a skill built up over a number of
years. The enjoyment and confidence built up can too easily
be spoilt by insistence on rewriting at the wrong moment.
Indeed, I have only known one junior age child who could
successfully revise her own work independently of the
teacher. The following poem comes from an outdoor lesson.
The children had to choose something, observe it, write
about it. Debbie wrote about a pair of stone angel's faces
carved on each side of the school's main entrance.

1st Attempt. Draft.

For years we have stood here.
Watching   Waiting.
Like spys.
(Ready to catch.)

2nd Draft.

For years we have waited
Waited to crumble into dust
We have watched children
*   come and go.*
We stand like spys.
Hidden in our cover of moss (and)
As silent as the air
We are left to rot.
Like a plant without water.
We are blind as moles.
And deaf as the sky
We are only stone.

3rd Draft.

We (have) will wait for years.
To crumble into dust.
Children come and go (through our
doors)
(We're) We stand like spys.
Hidden in our cover of grimy moss.
As silent as the air.
We are left to rot.
Like a plant without water.
We are as blind as moles.
(Yet we see death)
And deaf as the sky.
We are only stone.

Final draft.

We will wait for years
to crumble into dust.
Children come and go
But we remain.
We stand like spies
Hidden in our cover of grimy moss
As silent as the air.

We are like stars
Staring down at the earth.
We are left to crumble, wither,
Like a plant without water.
We are blind as moles
and deaf as the sky.
We are only stone.

Debbie Osman, 10 yrs.

It is fascinating to see how she trims lines to make them more effective.

> *For years we have stood here*

becomes,

> *For years we have waited*

then

> *We have waited for years*

and finally

> *We will wait for years.*

So too,

> *We have watched children come and go*

becomes

> *Children come and go.*

At one point she includes the line

> *We're like spies*

then alters *'We're'* to the powerful *'We stand'*. Her final images are crisp; nearly all natural –

> *As silent as the air.*
> *We are like stars . . .*
> *Like a plant without water . . .*
> *We are blind as moles*
> *. . . deaf as the sky.*

She gets rid of 'we are left to rot' and changes 'rot' in favour of 'crumble, wither'. At one point in the process she tries to write about something completely different but returns to her original idea. Such work is most unusual.

An earlier page shows her making notes while watching some workmen on the road.

> *torn up road*
> *people staring at the mess*
> *a blue car waiting for the lights to change*
> *a man making cement on the road*
> *An old granny walking by*
> *Opposite the fish bar*

> We are sitting
> A blind man in a suit walks by
> the toilet stand in the mess
> a truck driver up the road.

Back in the classroom she begins to work out her poem, barely referring back to her notes.

> the road like milk being churned
> children scurrying past
> Enormous yellow machines
> Like great metallic monsters
> Cars waiting at the traffic lights
> car horns hooting loudly
> Strong men are working/sweat drips from
>   foreheads
> The long desert like dusty road
> Is a modern mess

In the final draft she trims down her ideas for full effect, into what by now is becoming her own 'style'.

> Churned like milk
> Children scurry past.
> Great yellow machines
> Enormous metallic monster.
> Car horns hooting.
> Strong men work.
> Sweat drips from skin.
> The long dusty road.
> A modern mess.

Notice how in the final draft,

> The road like milk being churned

becomes

> Churned like milk.

> Children scurrying past the mess

becomes

> Children scurrying past.

She plays around with the words 'great' and 'enormous' to find their best place.

> Great/Enormous yellow machines
> like great metallic monsters

becomes

> Great yellow machines
> Enormous metallic monster

She reduces

> Cars waiting at the traffic lights
> car horns hooting loudly

to

Car horns hooting.
Strong men are working
becomes more succinctly
Strong men work
and so on.

This ability to redraft is exceptional. Most of us will start by
encouragement, and asking children to pick out the good bits
in their classmates writing, alerting individuals to strong and
weak parts when marking ... and working towards building
up this skill. How far it is taken depends on the teacher and
the class ... Perhaps you go to the point where you feel it
starts to interfere with their pleasure of writing.

● AS THEY FINISH WRITING

The children will all finish their pieces at different times, so it
is important to have something ready for them to 'get on
with' while you are still free to give help. Of course, there will
be times when you offer no help and let them get on with it –
and maybe one day a situation where help is not needed!
Once most of the children have finished I usually ask if anyone
wants to read their piece out. "Everyone reread your work to
yourself just to make sure that if you read it aloud there won't be
any bits that don't make sense or you can't read."

● MARKING

Now the finished poems have to be marked. The way in
which a piece is marked directly effects how the children will
write next time – after all, most children want to 'get it right'
and please their teacher. The sort of points we praise will be
repeated. Those we discourage may be dropped – if not – and
we find ourselves continually writing, "Handwriting poor",
then I suggest a new strategy is needed! After all, it is our job
to help children tackle their difficulties, not merely to point them
out. The child knows only too well that his or her handwriting
is poor, what is needed is help to overcome the difficulty.

Recently I visited a boys' prep school. In a 1st year junior class
I noticed a small boy sitting on his own, rather miserably
struggling with a story. The handwriting was diabolical ... I
looked back through his book and noticed that at the start of
the year his handwriting had been quite good but the teacher
had written, "Too slow – you must get more done." Similar
comments continued till the boy started to write more –
unfortunately in doing so he had to sacrifice his neat

handwriting and now the comments read: "Handwriting very poor – do something about it." No wonder he was miserable.

One object of marking must be to make sure that the next piece of writing improves. Look at the following poems and try to decide which you think is best. Which are the original lines, how closely observed are they, how perceptive, do the experiences seem real, did the writers enjoy writing them? Which words and phrases would you pick out as being well chosen, which are weak? Try to rework each poem yourself.

●   *Space Dragon*   **Night**

Outside cats screeching like babies.
The howl and barking of the dogs. Screaming of brakes as cars stop suddenly.

In space the darkness is pitch black. Like a night scenery, Like a gorilla's hand, stretching over the universe, like a cinema with no lights on. Like a black board with no writing on. In space the darkness is pitch black.

The noise of people shouting and screaming. "Look, can you see the moon glistening in the sky?" The stars sparkling and glittering.
The flashes of aeroplanes lights. "Can you hear footsteps of heavy feet and can you see the dark and creepy shadows moving across the wall?"

Naomi Blackman, 9 yrs.

Sarah Barrett, 9 yrs.

Each of these 4 poems is very different in approach but they all stem from the same lesson with a class of 3rd years who were well practised writers. The third piece, 'Darkness', was by a boy who had previously found writing a problem. Is it better than the ones above? Does comparing work like this help? Or should each piece be viewed individually as part of that child's own development?

●   Darkness

The grumbling mouth. Rock's thatching. The roof. I stumble in. I touch the cold clamy wall's. They hem you in. The utter blackness. Crowding me in. I could not even see my hand when I put it up to my face. The crannies letting a sparkle

of light in. The few
strand's of moss. The
amazement that Jesus
could arise. The cautious
footsteps, stopping and starting.
It seems like a nightmare.
My mind blank. A crack, a
Thud, an enormous rock
has fallen it proves that
it is insecure. My smallish
whisper echoes round the
hemming walls, it seems
like a shout. The scared
scream. The made foot-steps
echoing echoing my mind
is blank.

Jamie Lelliot, 9 yrs.

● **The Dead World**

A mist rises,
Leaving darkness,
The last heartbeat,
Echoes.
Through musty caves.
Rivers of streaming blood,
Running along the crevices,
Before me lies a world of mystery,
Woods and forests,
Are sprinkled,

With silver moonlight,
Trees stare at me,
Twigs crunch behind me,
But theres nobody there,
The moon's beam,
Reflects back on the dead,
Engraving their faces on the
trees,
Nothing exists,
Everything is dead.

Adrian Morris, 10 yrs.

Not all of us will have arrived with the same revised versions.
More importantly, we have all practised the skill of looking for
the weaknesses and strengths in pieces of writing with a view
to improving them. We have all tried to 'polish the poem'.

● **A FIRST AND SECOND RESPONSE**

The first response must be a serious consideration and
interest in the content – "I like this line", "These words fit
together well", "The ending is effective" – followed by some
suggestions on how to make the piece better – "What colour
is her hair", "How does she walk", "Can you say more about
the sound of her voice". When improvements have been
made by the child then it is time to make a 'fair copy' with the
punctuation correct, the grammar clear, the spelling right and

in neat handwriting. If our reaction is a furious yell of "the handwriting is appalling" – then the children will think that you are only interested in how neatly written the piece is and all their efforts will be channelled into writing neatly, not caring about the words and ideas they use. The idea of a rough copy is quite an accepted practice with adults – indeed it is what I am doing at this very moment and I expect this will be rewritten 4 or 5 times before I feel it says what I want it to say.

● **A PLAN OF ATTACK**

Read each piece twice – once for a reaction to the content, once for a reaction to the surface errors. Firstly, as someone who will give praise and make helpful suggestions, secondly as an 'editor' who will help with the finer details.

1 The 'overall' reaction.

Use the child's name: *I like this, Jason.*

Mention a piece you liked: *The piece about the sun was good ...*

Ask questions: *How did you feel?*
Was this a sad time?

Comments such as: *I always enjoy reading your work –* if meant – are well worth the few seconds it takes to write them.

2 Look at the 'good' bits.

Tick the words and phrases that are well used. In the following poem I have marked the words that I find particularly successful.

● **The Storm**

*First a **lash** of lighting*
***licks** the **lilac** clouds.*
The thunder smashes like sauce
pans clattering together.
*A **muscular rein** of lightning*
***punches** the **static** ground.*
*The icy rain **grips** against the window*
as it pours to the earth.

Richard, 8 yrs.

The words 'lash', 'licks' and 'lilac' seem particularly effective – they alliterate, are powerful, reflecting the sudden ferocity of the lightning. The word 'licks' reminds me of the words 'flick' and 'flicker', they echoed in my head as I read it. The colour lilac is unusual yet appropriate for a thundery evening. It makes it seem more ominous. But 'The saucepans clattering' is a clichéd idea – certainly thunder never sounds like that. He continues to write more powerfully about the lightning. 'A muscular rein' is an unusual combination of words – certainly lightning can 'punch' the ground – which is 'static'. Is using 'static' stating the obvious? Does he use static because he is thinking of static electricity or is it to emphasise the contrast between the static earth and the sudden movement of the lightning? Can a 'rein' punch something? Would 'lashes' or 'whips' have been better words? ... He really has thought hard over this and concentrated a lot of images into a small space. Finally, the rain 'grips' against the window – an arresting idea that makes the storm seem more alive, more desperate, more menacing. The final line in contrast seems weak.

Our responses will be individual and will vary but the important thing is to encourage the children to try out new words, new ideas, to think ... Inevitably an adventurous approach will lead to errors but errors should be seen as an invaluable part of development. They are the testing ground for new ideas, often producing unique imagery, as when Jamie describes dawn:

> The dawn spotted by the
> cockrel laver twisting round.

When I asked him what he meant he said that he was thinking that a cockrel's colours were like the sunrise. Though incorrectly spelt, he has broken the rules of grammer to produce a startling but beautifully true image that is quite unique.

3 Look at the *'weak'* bits.

Having ticked the good parts now underline a few – or all – of the weak parts. When the work is returned an underlined word alerts the child to a weakness for them to reconsider. Examples can be read aloud for class discussion and suggestions for alternatives made. In the end it is left to the writer to choose whether he will make a change or defend his original idea. Remember that too many underlinings will produce a sense of failure. Beware!

●　　　　**SOME WEAKNESSES TO LOOK FOR**

a When children start writing they often make their descriptions too bare:

> The farmer chased the fox.

We should encourage children at this stage to fill out their ideas with more description.

> The fat-faced farmer chased the sly fox.

So, often children will be sent back to their places to add more words.

b But too often the words chosen are poor choices – words taken from the surface level of vocabulary. 'Come', 'go' and 'move' are big offenders.

The big slug moved along the moving branch.

It is not a very good idea to change the words yourself. Here, I would underline the weaker words, where I felt the child had not *thought* about the choice of words, and ask him to try to find a 'better' word. If the child is stuck you might suggest 3 or 4 words yourself, or ask for class suggestions, and then let him choose.

The fat slimy slug slithered along the trembling branch.

c If a word is repeated it often means that the writer couldn't be bothered to select the right word and has merely put down the first thing that came into his head. Remember the 'big' shark?

d Sometimes it is not a matter of adding words, but rather the sentences and ideas themselves are too brief. When recounting an event, children often leave parts out. This may be because their sense of fantasy is strong and they seem unaware that others have not taken part in it.

The cat moved.

could be extended –

The slender cat slipped through deep shadows.

Question the child. Point out that they haven't mentioned enough. The reader needs to know more.

e There may come a point when the children use too many words – particularly adjectives and present participles.

The one-eyed, shabby, down at heel, tired, weary cat
slipping, sliding, slithering along the wall . . .

Often in a situation like this the words work against each other. Sometimes they merely mean the same and therefore only one word should be selected ('tired' and 'weary' for instance). When children start writing they usually need to be encouraged to add more. Later on they have to be encouraged to pare down their writing. It is a matter of choosing only the words you need and not adding words for the sake of using them. Search for words with similar meanings and the statement of the obvious.

The flowing current of the moving river.

Here the words 'flowing' and 'moving' are unnecessary – after all, the word 'current' implies that the river flows and moves. It is rather like saying 'the cold ice' or 'the hot sun'. Avoid overstatement – a cut can all too soon become a torrent or gushing lava! Bring them back to saying what it is really like, to observing the truth of the experience.

f Where children have forced a rhyme they may be setting themselves an impossibly hard task that leads to dishonesty and often complete nonsense. A few older children may try using rhymes and find themselves good enough word-searchers to use it with some effect.

●   **Devastation**

The hovering sound	Laser flies
Cities fry	Saucers peer
Trembling underground	Like hidden spies
A burning sky.	While spacecraft seer.
Buildings crumble	Nothing spared
Paving cracks	Towns are dead
Humans humble	The forces scared
Drop like sacks.	Nothing said.

Steven Wood, 9 yrs.

Compare the following poems, both by Darren. Where are the weak points? What advice would you give about the repetition of idea in lines 4 and 6 of 'Silk'? Do the poems read well – or does he need to listen more closely to the rhythm? Would you praise or discourage these attempts from a nine year old?

●   **Dragons**

Slithery slimy long but thin
The dragons tail is this
He who smiles with a terrible grin
and who laughs with a terrible hiss.

With humps on his back and side
And fire breathing nostrils flared wide
the gargoyle 20 feet long
Starts singing his carnivorous song.

Flesh and skin to eat
He'll gobble up any meal
this terrible and gluttonous beast
starts eating his luscious feast.

But did he really live
and was he really our foe
with humps on his back and side
and nowhere now to go?

Darren O'Byrne, 9 yrs.

Silk

The spiders web hangs from the dust.
Outside the house old metals rust
as fallen leaves lay on the ground
the spider's camp just might be found,
Yet in all these things that have no use
a spider's web might just be found.
The spider spins transparent threads.
This sticky stuff the fly it dreads.
This fragile web made out of silk
could be destroyed with just a jilt,
so delicate, a silver lace,
made by an artist full of grace.

Darren O'Byrne, 9 yrs.

Half rhymes ('wine' and 'dine' for instance) will occur quite by
accident in children's writing. So too, will internal rhymes –
rhymes that occur within the poem and not at the end of the
lines.

*Take a **match***
***scratch** it against the box...*

Most children will naturally alliterate:

Lingering lazy ladies lay cemented
to the golden sand.

Furthermore, if they are word-searching they will use
'onomatopoeia' – words whose sounds complement the
thing they describe, such as hiss, scratch, squeak, click, crack,
squelch. All these are writers' 'techniques' that we learnt
about at school. Children use them quite naturally. When
used you can draw the children's attention to them,
explaining how they can add life to a piece of writing. By
doing so, you will find that they start to use them
purposefully for good effect. Exercises in such 'devices' can
be devised for fun but should not be overemphasised as they
may lead to children forcing alliteration in the same way that
rhymes can be forced to produce false writing effects.

g Flowery 'poetic' language and old-fashioned words should
be avoided – such as 'morn', 'yore', 'thou'.

h Is the author writing honestly from his or her own
experience? It is so much easier to write truthfully and vividly
of an account of snow in the playground than it is to write of
polar bears and penguins in the antarctic – after all, we've
never even been there, how can we hope to describe it?
(Though it is true to say that we can use our own experience
to forge links with experiences we have not had to create

some sort of understanding – for instance, we might use an experience of being shut in a cupboard as a child to create a link with the experience of being shut in a dark cell.) Above all, has the writer used his senses to discover the true nature of the experience?

i Avoid clichés – what we are looking for is where children have thought of new images, considering each word, not idly borrowing stale ideas – 'blue seas that sparkle' (when many British seas are dull grey), 'blankets of snow' or 'fluffy cotton wool clouds' are favourites. Tell the children that these ideas have already been used and that you want **their own** ideas – not someone else's.

j Has the author 'waffled' or does the passage have a direct, dramatic impact. Which of these two beginnings to a piece on 'fire' makes a better beginning for a poem.

> *'As I was by the bonfire I was watching*
> *and when they were putting a light to it*
> *if I looked closely I could see a flame*
> *leap up a branch.'*

or

> *'Flames leapt. We stared into the fire.'*

The second beginning strikes me as being far more direct and dramatic. This is partly because of the *short* sentences and partly because we move directly to the main points. We can discuss 'beginnings' and 'endings' – dramatic beginnings and endings that do not rely on waking up and finding it was all a dream. If an ending cannot be found it is usually best to merely end the piece with a strong, final line and no intention of 'tying it up' or indeed 'explaining'.

k Words can be trimmed to have more impact.

> *The blood was pouring from his arm*

becomes

> *Blood poured from his arm.*

l If the poem's pattern seems inappropriate or the poem looks like chopped up prose you can either show the child where you might put in the lines or ask her to write it out as prose. To help them improve with making patterns you can:

1 *Pin up successful examples.*
2 *Put varied examples on the board for handwriting practice.*
3 *Make up class poems on the board.*
4 *Explain that the break falls so that each line makes sense on its own.*
5 *Say that each new idea starts on a new line.*
6 *Finally, let them read their classmates work, "See how John does it" and poems by established authors.*

Some children find that they are happier writing prose. Let them ... As long as it is well done, for most of our 'poetry rules and techniques' can equally apply to prose.

m Is the poem complete? Or has the author tired ...? Is the meaning clear, does it logically unfold, is it structured to hold our interest? Hard tasks for young children.

Yet when writing short pieces (as opposed to stories) a unity is often naturally achieved especially where

1 *They wrote swiftly, with an unbroken flow.*
2 *They have discussed and worked on the experience through other areas of the curriculum – art, drama, science or topic.*

Early poems can be structured for the children as you collect the words. So when collecting words about a bonfire, organise the collecting in a certain order that will give their writing a structure – the flames, the sounds, the sparks, the smoke, the shadows cast and the ashes in the morning. Such grouping might form your structure.

n Finally, is the poem a report of an event or is it a recreation of the experience? If it is a report send the child back to add 'details', using all five senses.

●   **AT LAST, THE SURFACE ERRORS**

Now tackle the surface errors – capital letters, punctuation, spelling, grammatical accuracy, handwriting.... Again, some, children's enthusiasm is dampened by the sight of virtually every word 'corrected'. Select what to concentrate on according to each individual.

The child can now have her work returned to look at or to copy up as a revised, neat version for poetry collection.

●   **FOLLOWING THE LESSON UP**

To show the children that you value their work and to add an incentive to boost their concentrated efforts, there are a number of ways of following up a writing lesson.

a *Read the poem to the class, other classes, in assembly or in the school 'show'.*
b *Make a poster for wall display.*
c *Add it to the child's own booklet or class scrapbook.*
d *Send child and poem to the Head.*
e *Make a fair copy to go home.*
f *Enter poems for class magazine or school magazine.*
g *Send poems to local paper or radio station.*
h *Enter competitions – W.H. Smith's Young Writers, Cadbury's Poetry*

Competition, the Poetry Society's 'Young Poets' Competition, Schools Poetry Association Competitions, etc.

i Invite a writer into school through your local Arts Association's 'Writers In Schools' scheme or the Poetry Society's 'Poets In Schools' scheme.

● A CREATIVE SCHEME?

The ideas in this book have been presented stage by stage, not because they should necessarily be followed as a scheme but because certain ideas are more suitable for older children as they contain more complex linguistic twists than others. So, anyone with a 4th year class of junior children will be able to use all the ideas in this book with some success, but those with younger children should be careful to present ideas taken from stages three or four in a fashion appropriate to the younger children. Indeed, some ideas from stage four would certainly not work with top infants. Furthermore, those ideas should only form a beginning for class writing work. I hope that once the teacher has grasped the two approaches, he or she will be able to adapt them to different situations and children, building up their own store of ideas. However, the ideas alone will not magically help children to develop their writing. The teacher has to engage him or herself imaginatively in the task of encouraging self-analysis without discouraging the child. This is done by an attitude that offers help rather than just negative criticism, that expects the best and enjoys and respects each individual child in its own right.

Whereas you can wander into a 4th year class of junior children, fire a writing idea at them and come out an hour later with a bunch of good poems, this does not apply so readily to top infants and lower juniors. These children will need more build up, discussion work, word collecting over a period of time, topic work around the subject using the appropriate language, drama, model work, drawing and painting. All these activities help to develop the child's vocabulary and ability to use words appropriately in the correct context, as well as helping him or her to symbolise the experience internally before expressing it on paper. Some examples in this book show faults. Not many children's poems do not. However, to give an idea of the range of results to expect from the average child, as well as the more gifted, we have purposely included some example poems with weaknesses.

● HOW OFTEN?

Children get good at writing by writing. Some form of writing should be done every day where the children are actively engaged in the process and not merely answering textbook questions – reports, jokes, sketches, conversations, playlets, observations, personal events, views, arguments, stories, chapters, poems, diaries, ideas.... How often your class will use a poetry idea depends on your emphasis and how strongly you believe that children get better at writing by writing and not by answering text books.

If the teacher enjoys teaching children to write, and puts it over enthusiastically then the children soon begin to value what they are doing. Writing poetry engages them in a directly personal way that most other work ignores. It is an expression of *their views* and therefore a direct extension of *their personality*.... With confidence in writing and a sense of achievement come a personal gain. It is one lesson where they are asked to create new ideas from themselves. It is no coincidence when the end of term comes that the children want to take home their poetry folders above all other books.

It is important to provide a balance and wide variety of different writing tasks, for different readers – not merely a diet of poetry. After all, some children respond better to other modes of writing.

Children soon become aware of the differences between different types of writing. Stories have their own problems particularly of action and plot. A story has things happening in it. Poems have their own rules to obey. This distinction becomes clearer the more they write and the more they have read to them. Our experience is that one of the main values of word searching is that it enhances all of a child's writing.

●   **BUT IT DIDN'T WORK**

All classes are different, each day is different. Some days the chemistry is just not right and what has worked for years flops. You will need to pick, choose, develop, adopt, adapt, add and alter our ideas to suit your pupils' needs and your situation. Remember that our approach is developmental. This means that your first results may be disappointing. It takes time for the children to develop their writing skills.

●   **TEACHING DIFFERENT AGE GROUPS?**

With different ages a different approach has to be adopted – though the underlying principles of observing and discussing will be the same. Infants tend to write written speech – juniors should be encouraged to refine their ideas. With infants it is important to work closely at their level of fantasy. For instance, you could pretend that a gnome has granted you 3 wishes and you want them to whisper to you the 3 craziest wishes they can think of for you to write down. Each writing lesson should be a surprise so that they can't guess what's coming next.

Initially infants will be brought together to observe, talk and select a few words to describe an experience. Later they can sit round the teacher whose questioning can stimulate ideas. These can be written up by the teacher and reread as they go along. The following poem describing a witch was made up in this way. I told the class that I had met a witch last night and that we were going to describe her ... "What colour was her hat? What shape was it? What did her face look like? What colour were her eyes? What was her nose like? ..." I had previously made a list to base my questions on – to describe the hat, face, eyes, nose, teeth, hair, chin, cloak, hands, fingernails, what she holds, her cat, what she is doing and what noises she makes. The second poem was written in the same way after looking at a candle with a small group of middle infants.

● **Witch poem**

A triangular black hat,
a crooked face,
horrible black eyes,
a long bending nose,
sharp dirty green teeth.
Flies snakes and spiders
creeping in her black tatty
twisted curly hair.
A pointed chin
with a black beard.
A black cloak
covered with zig zags.

Pointed long green hands
purple fingernails
like a cats claws.
Holding a sharp knife
and her wand.
Beside her on the grass
sits her cat R2 D2
softly purring.
She stamps
a crooked green hobble.
I hear
a noisy bad cackle.

Class poem by middle infants.

● *About a candle*

The candle stays alight.
The flame is still.
The yellow flame wiggles all the time.
The wind blows it.
The orange flame flickers.
The black wick burns.
The wick is curly.
The tip is light orange,

like a giraffe's neck.
The white wax slides
down to the bottom.
It is like a bubble, round.
Smooth, hot wax hardens.
Melted wax like fat
drips down the candle.
Like a straight stick,
like a yellow pipe,
The candle burns.
Mary Anne puffed.
The flame blew away.
Grey smoke whispers, wizzles, whizzes,
drifts into the air.

Brian, Teresa, Mary Anne, Michelle, 5–6 yrs.

Later, infants can write their own sentences.

Sounds middle infants

Crash!
A car driving and it crashed into a wall.
Bang!
Somebody banged their head on a wall.
An arrow popped into the balloon.
Crunch!
Kevin crunched a biscuit.
Tom crunched a crunchy crisp.
Shuffle!
The wind shuffled the leaves.
Whisper!
A whispering in your ear.
Someone whispers about having sweets but they are joking.
The whistling wind blowing away the black clouds.
Rattle!
A baby rattles a red rattle.
Trickle!
A red jelly wobbles.
Chatter!
Matthew chatters about his mum.
Moan!
A black and white cow moans and sneezes.

I like the sound of red aeroplanes flying to the beach.
I like the sound of Matthews feet clumping in my
    mum's kitchen.

I like the sound of a small green rocket shooting up in
the air to the moon.
I like the sound of the wind whistling through the
town.
I like the sound of my mum eating crunchy sweets.
I like hearing the horses shoes clonking and
clattering down the windy streets.

Matthew Murphy/Paul Hill/Michelle Finnigan/
Karen Groombridge/Teresa Groombride/
Brian Blanchett, 5–6 yr olds.

Essentially, the same notions of word searching and
observation lie behind all the work at whatever level. Younger
children will need more support. Older children will use more
challenging writing ideas, their discussions may focus more
on form and ideas rather than collecting words. Young
children write better if they have worked at an experience for
longer in different areas of the curriculum – dance, drama,
music, art and topic work in particular.

Whatever the age remember that for some children it may
take 1, 2, 3 or more terms to develop their work to satisfy your
highest expectations ... This requires great patience, the
ability to bounce back with another idea, to keep
encouraging, not to give up and to remember that one day
you will kindle that creative fire that everyone has. And if your
expectations are high some children will reach a point where
they can sit down and write successfully about whatever *they*
want to write about.

● **A SERIOUS GAME**

It is never easy to say what it is that creates an atmosphere
where children write creatively – An enjoyment of what each
individual has to offer, a love of words, a rich and exciting use
of language, an encouraging attitude so that children start to
change their self image, to feel that they can do it. Above all, it
is probably the ability of the teacher to turn the whole activity
into a serious game. A game that is both fun and fulfilling.
This will go a long way towards developing a love of writing
and enchancing our children's lives with a clearer expression
of the true nature of themselves and their world.

Pie Corbett

● **THE SENSES**

This is a series of 5 lessons on the senses, listing our likes and dislikes. They should perhaps not be done immediately after each other. The ideas can be listed as those we like or hate.

I would introduce each lesson by discussing the sense, what it might be like without it, what we would miss and what the dangers would be. Ask round the class to find likes and dislikes. Make a list of words to use for this sense. It is a good idea to have made your own list beforehand and by questioning prompt the class towards remembering words they may miss out.

Sometimes you will find the children only write rather short, dull sentences

'I like the sound of cars'.

You can stop the class and point out that this is not interesting enough. What are the cars doing, what sound do they make, what colour are they ...

'I like the sound of red cars roaring up the road'.

Children should not aim for a long list of short sentences but a list of 6/7 ideas that are interesting and fleshed out with good words. A class collage poster can be made with drawings of things we like, cuttings from magazines ...

● **Taste Word List**

spicy sugary salty bitter creamy watery dry icy sweet wet sour milky sickly strong weak sharp lemon earthy minty tasteless fizzy tang flavour oily crisp crunch chew gobble greedy curry acid vinegar peppery malt onions garlic.

● **Smells Word List**

smell fragrance tang sniff inhale scent dank stale rancid perfume drift waft rise unpleasant odour bad foul rank fetid incense

Outdoors – *Roses, sea, dead fish, apples, hops, tarmac, sweat.*
Indoors – *Shoe polish, bacon, kippers, Harpic, soap, coffee.*
Unusual – *Pages of a new book, felt tips, moth balls, pot pourri, car seats.*
Burning – *Bonfires, coal, cigars, old fireworks, barbeque.*

● *Sounds*

The boom of a door breaks the silence.
The cackle of a witch in the night air giggling to herself.
The chattering and murmuring of Mum downstairs.
The crunch of the crisp pack being thrown away in the bin.
The moan of an old man grumbling.
The squeal of brakes skidding furiously.
The cold wind that whips the sunlight from the trees.
The steady hum of children working.
The clatter of the dustbin falling over.
The dribble of a tap not turned off.
The gurgle and groan as the bath water gushes and swirls
    down the drain.
                    Group Poem

● *Touch*

I feel the hot and smooth pebble on the beach,
            the damp fur of a cat,
            the tickle of an ant crawling up my leg.
I feel the slippery skin of a slug,
            the softness of my dog's fur between my fingers,
            the roughness of stones on my hands and feet.
I feel the jagged edges of a baked bean tin,
            the cool and smooth milk bottle,
            the rough brick of a wall.
I feel the coldness of winter upon me,
            the frost in my fingers,
            the slippery bumpy icy crystals.
I feel the wind drifting and groaning,
            the cold, smooth surface of someone's tombstone
            the coffin that I will die in.
                    Group Poem

● *Looking*

I like to look at the dogs playing on a summer's day.
I like to look at a windmill twisting and turning.
I like to look at the water, it's like a mirror.
I like to look at flowers glazing in the sun.   Group Poem

● **FIVE LIES**

– – – – – – – – – – – – – – – – – – – –

Many of us encounter lies at an early age. We all know that in
most circumstances to lie is wrong. Children like the idea of

being invited to lie. You could list some subjects to write about – *sun, sea, clouds, mirror, rock, comb, cats, rain, snow, elastic* . . . – and ask them to write down 5 sentences, each one a different lie. They can lie about its shape, size, colour, feel, smell, taste or function.

A good way to start this lesson is to go round the class giving children an object (grass) and asking them to tell one lie about it (the grass is fat as an elephant's foot).

Children enjoy hearing these poems read aloud at the end of the lesson.

● **Five lies about the sun**

The sun has watery eyes.
It pours down silk blood
that drips on your soaking head.
The sun has a light ginger beard.
The sun is a sharp triangle.
It is made of brilliant fudge.

Group Poem

● **BODY SOUNDS**

– – – – – – – – – – – – – – – – – – – –

This idea originally came from a line in a child's poem and some extraordinary photographs in a colour supplement of microscopic bugs and areas of skin magnified many thousands of times.

Did your class know that living in their eyebrows there are microscopic insects! What would different body movements sound like to them? We don't hear our eyelids closing but to a tiny mite it would be a tremendous sound. Make two lists on the board – one for different parts of the body and the other for 'sound' words (*crunch, crack, click, squeak, squeal* . . .). Ask the children to write down different sounds that parts of the body might make using the phrase **'Listen, can you hear the sound of** . . .' to link the poem up. As with most writing sessions it may be helpful to read several examples to the class before they start writing. It is important to choose carefully the models that you read to the class as these set a standard for them to aim at, and act as a stimulus to the imagination. Often you will have to write your examples yourself . . . and may want to write alongside the class. To display these poems a large poster can be made in the shape of a skeleton with the poem written onto it.

Body Sounds

Listen –
Can you hear the
sound of the
bones grinding,
the soft beat of my heart,
the constant flowing of my blood,
the squeak of my nails
as they scrape
around my skin,
The swell of my lungs
and rolling of my tongue swirling
around my mouth
The blood seeping
through my veins,
The sound of my heart punching
the blood away
and the
moaning of the
bones.   Asleep.
Silent.   Only
the pump pumping
of my
heart.

Katya Haine, 7 yrs.

Listen –

Can you hear
  the bones creaking
a silent murmur
  rustling in the forest
little creatures
  crawling everywhere
and rummaging around my
  hair grunting crunching
tumbling
  as they fall down
the hill
  chattering as
they go.
  The gurgling fizz
as lemonade
  rumbles down
my throat
  moaning grumbling
blasting
  as the food
rumbles down
  swirling swerving
rolling as the blood
  tumbles round my body.

Jacqueline Collins, 7 yrs.

● **BONFIRES AND CANDLES**

– –

Here are two contrasting lessons. Bonfires can be tackled in
November when most children have the chance to
experience the thrill of a large fire. Make a large word
collection about a bonfire seen on a dark night – what colours
can you see, how do the flames move, what sounds does the
fire make, what is happening to the wood, what is coming out
of the top of the fire, what will be left in the morning? Bonfire
poems can be illustrated by felt-tip, paints, or by cutting out
red tissue flames. Often children will want to add fireworks
and guys.

Candles are quiet and soft compared to the raging bonfire. These poems can be written inside the shape of a candle. Ask the children to write down their own list of words, reminding them to think of the shape, colour, flame, wax and shadows. Having been marked for spellings this list can be put straight into the candle shape. They can be cut out and hung onto card, one each side, and suspended as mobiles.

●

The Candles

Two dead
candles
Still in the
dark –
a match cracks and
lights.
It brings the
candles
to life. One is a
Lord
and the other
bows
like a servant.
Joy
to them.
They
dance.

Karen Venton, 7 yrs.

Fire

The fire is lit
and the room
gets warmer and brightens
up,
at first a very little fire
burns then it boils
and blazes with life.
The flickering flames
of a fierce fire
flare in the darkness.
The flames greedily gobble
up the wood.
The wood crackles and cries
as the furious flames of fire devour
them up.
The flames spread as if
they were the
clouds spreading over the
dark misty sky.

Hayley Kemp, 8 yrs.

●   *The Candle*

The candle shines like a golden sun.
The fierce cells of burnt colours
  gleaming and blazing.
The cells of colours are fierce and leaping
The pouncing candle-light leaps high over
  the pounding wax candles.
The blazing fire burns through
  the centre of the flames.
The flickering beams scatter the ashes
  left on the ground like a body.
The prisoned fire is surrounded like
  a leap of wind.
The flame is lit with the sound
  of wonder.

       Lisa Smith, 8 yrs.

49

This lesson can be left to the appropriate moment. Get the children to look closely at how it falls and what it is like on the ground – this will help them avoid such words as 'nice' and 'lovely'.

List words describing how the snow falls, how it settles, its colour, what it feels like, what it does to houses, trees puddles, what it is like to walk through, what happens when the sun strikes it and it turns to slush. Try to encourage them to avoid the Christmas card clichés (blanket of snow) and keep to the cold realities of snow and ice.

An interesting display can be made with white cut-outs of snow crystal shapes on black sugar paper with the poems stuck between them.

If they finish quickly, let them write a poem about an icicle inside an icicle shape – they write a word list to describe the shape, the feel, what it is like and then they slot this list into the shape.

●

Icicle

The sharp jaggered
icicle hangs from
    the barn's roof
it is crystal clear
it is as sharp
    as a dagger
    it is
    the hang-
    ing icicle
    of death.

Kerry Colbran, 8 yrs.

Snow

**Flitters, flutters,
Icy puddles,
Clear as glass,
Lace on twigs.
Tree shed heavy load
Springs back to soldier,
Hooves of horse,
Hoof prints in snow,
Muddy boots,
Icicles drip,
Snow melts to slush,
Streams trickle away.**

Kerry Colbran, 8 yrs.

● **Snow**

*It grips on roofs.
It camouflages trees, it makes a quick disguise.
The snow covers the world like a massive sheet.
The wind bitterly bites into your flesh, it
tosses the snow all around the town.
Icicles form on the roof edges and window
panes, someone breaks one and it shatters into*

tiny fragments, it splinters.
Suddenly a blaze of sun-light sheets through
the clouds.

Julian Thomas, 8 yrs.

● *Snow*

The snow drifts down to the ground.
Covering everything in sight.
Sculpting trees,
moulding the edges of houses.
Icicles hang from window ledges,
as if the house had teeth.
Snow crunches as you tread on it.
Wind whispers down chimneys,
carrying snow with it.
Snow smothers gardens,
parks and houses.
Snow stops falling.
Everything is silent.
Snowmen in gardens melt away,
as the snow disappears.
Everywhere is wet and muddy,
where the snow had fallen.

Jenny Humphries, 8 yrs.

● **TO BE ALONE ...**

What is it like to be alone? Imagine that you are lying on top
of a hill, the blazing summer sun beating down, a skylark
calling far above, blue sky stretches to the horizon,
occasionally clouds drift by ... you close your eyes and your
thoughts float like the clouds through your mind. Write down
your thoughts and feelings, what you can hear, feel, see....

Sometimes it is pleasant to be alone, if you can create the
right atmosphere of a dreamy summer's day for your class,
take their ideas beyond a description of their surroundings
and write about their feelings too.

Sadly enough, many children know that being alone is not
always a pleasant experience.... Many of us have lain awake
at night, listening to muffled conversations from the kitchen,

hearing the wind beat rain against the window pane and watched shadows on the walls. There are many other occasions when your class may have been alone – waiting for a parent to pick them up from school, standing on the edge of the playground, staring into the bars of the electric fire at night. Ask them to choose a time when they were alone – what were they thinking, what could they see, hear, feel? Ask them to close their eyes and remember what it felt like.

A simple way to write about loneliness is to use the phrase, 'To be alone is like . . .' and complete the image. Strangely, this is an ideal that can work well with quite young children. As a stimulus to writing play them some music to write by.

●

To Be Alone

To be alone is like being
in a grave
in the earth.
Like a
star floating
in
space slowly moving.
To be alone is
like standing
in a dark room holding
a
stick.
To be alone is
like
one word closed inside
a book.
To be alone is
like a soul
of a man hiding in
the trees.

Matthew Cole, 7 yrs.

Alone

To be alone not alone
Sounds come creeping in
because behind closed
doors all is still
Behind closed doors is
sadness
The sunset out of
the window
brightens the room
The curtains were
hanging
To be alone
To speak in silence
nothing in the room
The January winds
were blowing
Behind closed doors

The stars in the sky
drift
The stars turn grey then
black and blue
rain began to fall
Clouds were drifting
one by one
Silent whispering
The tiny drops
of water

To be alone is much too much.

Lisa Smith, 8 yrs.

● NIGHT

- - - - - - - - - - - - - - - - - - - -

Darkness is often a vivid fear that children write well about.
You can discuss what it is like to be in the dark of your
bedroom. List words to describe the darkness, shadows, the
shapes, the night outside, the sounds, the feelings, and
eventually, sleep.

It is a good idea to discuss, ask for ideas and focus on vivid
words to use. Try to avoid 'Dracula' and discuss what it is
really like lying in the darkness of their bedroom. It is not
enough to say that 'it is creepy'. To be effective the children
will have to describe the dark room so that the reader feels it
is creepy without being told so.

● *Night*

The night is drifting back once again
covering everything it touches
with a funereal suit of black.
A shadow swooping an outline
of a candle flickering in the
moonlight a blurry figure
suspiciously walking down an unknown lane.

Jamie Lelliott, 9 yrs.

● Shadow

The evening creeps nearer, every shadow
elongates and looks forever colder
and forever blacker,
sliding, slithering, leaping round every
curve and corner
drowns every light
suspiciously stretching
silently strange shapes emerge
like great monsters appearing and
disappearing in a strange mist
steadily sneeking like
lizards hunting for their
prey, known as light to us.

Neil Thatcher, 9 yrs.

This involves making a list of things you are afraid of. Try to avoid too many stereotypes. In the discussion, ask round for a variety of fears – perhaps starting with some of your own.

● *Darkness*

I am afraid
of dark gloomy
trees, hands spreading
all over me, eyes
staring all around,
feet stamping
me to the the ground.

I am afraid
of cranes,
spears pointing
at me, fierce
monsters all around me.

I am afraid
of shadows on
the wall creeping
towards me.

I am afraid
of heights when
I look down
it might make me fall.

I am afraid
of stray dogs
barking at me
and growling.

I am afraid
of dark in the
room, I can see
nothing but pitch
black dark.

Jacqueline Collins, 7 yrs.

● **WIND**

This should be a forceful poem with plenty of strong words – like the wind itself. Think about the sounds the wind makes and what it does to things. What does it feel like when it blows against you? Describe how the trees, a newspaper, smoke, a washing-line might move. What do people and animals do? And when the wind stops blowing what can you hear? What does it feel like.

This poem can look effective if the children write it in a pattern as if the wind were pushing the words.

● *Wind*

The whirling wind squeals and rattles around the chimney
The hiss and rustling as it blows and howls through

the trees.
It bustles and hurls through the key hole, tending to
make the door creak and shake.
The wind bellows, groans, screeches through the grass
leaves, waste packets roll tumble and glide in parties
down and along the street.
It stings, sharply slings and cuts the skin. It slices
and tears your clothes and makes your hair
stand on end.

Deborah Blanchett, 8 yrs.

● OLD AGE

– –

This lesson could start by concentrating on an old person's
hands, face, the sound of the voice, his or her movements.
The words you collect will generally be applicable to most old
people. You can then be more specific and perhaps talk about
an old person the children know. Encourage the class to think
about the clothes old people wear, their rooms, hobbies or
habits, mannerisms, stories they repeat, quirks of speech and
incidents that typify the old person they are thinking of.

My Gran

**My gran creeps about on our
old brown floor, she is very old. Her
hands are wrinkled she has patterns
on her face. The patterns are like
mazes. Her back is like a hump.
Her voice is like a crow laughing.
She is weak and feeble. Her knees
are bent. She says 'Hello my
darlings. How are you today?'**

Amanda Cornwell, 8 yrs.

My Grandad

*My Grandad has blood
    shot eyes, spider
web eyes, he has not
    got long to live.
Everybody in the street feels
    sorry for him.*

He watches football
every week.
He supports Brighton as he
lives there.
Every time he touches
me I can feel his
bony hands.
I like to visit
my Grandad. He is
so kind.

Sherriff Anjourin,
8 yrs.

My Nan

Like a restless big bat,
a buzzing bee,
like a jumping jelly bean,
like a dustpan and brush.
If in front of a lot of
     washing she starts to jump.
Like a long lost horse,
like a war dance with only one person.
like an uncontrollable hen,
like a pair of dancing shoes.
a bird building a nest,
like a dragon giving no one
     a chance to rest,
like a tired out donkey,
like a restless old nanny goat
from morning till night.

Rachel Smith, 10 yrs.

One

I wish I was

a green scaly turtle swimming in the Indian Ocean

a huge African elephant stamping through the steaming jungle.

Try to encourage the fullest possible picture using plenty of describing words.

Two

It's a secret, but ...

Letting someone in on a lot of secrets about yourself.

It's a secret but I live in a dragon's cave.

It's a secret but I sometimes take a giraffe for a walk.

Three

Perfect

I dreamed I was a typewriter that never printed a wrong letter.

I dreamed I was a table and never rocked.

I dreamed I was a bin and nothing tipped into me.

Four

That was the day

when something weird and wonderful happened.

That was the day when the flowers started dancing.

That was the day when Tarzan swung backwards.

That was the day when a martian was washing in my bath.

Five

The quiet me

Think carefully of all the times of the day (and night) when you are quiet.

I'm quiet when I'm puzzling out the largest jigsaw puzzle in the house.

I'm quiet when I'm working on division, I'm quiet when I'm thinking about a really difficult sum.

Six

The Iron Man

Based on the book by Ted Hughes. Part one should be a description of the Iron Man while part two should tell us what he eats.

- His eyes swivel like searchlights,
  his heart pounds and echoes like a
  blacksmith's anvil.
- His legs take the weight of houses.
- He chews through strands of rusty barbed
  wire,
  He crunches old cars like crackers. etc.

Seven   **Dreams**
- A shoe dreams of being worn by a princess.
- A door dreams of not being a door because it
  is always slammed.
- A snowman dreams that the sun will never
  shine.

Eight   **Birthday list/Christmas sack**
- Making up a list of strange presents.
- – a train made out of fire,
- a tree with heads,
- a box of wind,
- a map of darkness.

Nine   **The building site**
- Try to visit a building site. Plenty of scope for
  onomatopoeia. List the sounds made by the
  different machines on the site. Listen to the
  men at work. Use some of the language of the
  building site in your poem.
- Voices bellow, hands signal, grinding of the
  cement mixer, whirring, humming, clanging,
  screeching of brakes . . .

Ten   **To a gnome**
- Imagine what huge objects must look like to
  something small.
- To a gnome a road is a giant runway where
  terrifying shapes speed past.
- To a gnome the side of a house is a cliff that
  can't be climbed.

● **FOG**

Though 'Fog' may seem a clichéd subject for creative writing, it is nevertheless a good one. How does fog move, what colour is it, what does it feel like, what happens to sounds in it, what do people do when it comes and would you feel alone in it?

● *Fog*

A thick, misty, dust lumbers along. Snuffling through
the hedges.
Tickling the cobwebs as it trickles, sneakily down
the window pane.
Pure white fragments forming, camouflaging, transferring
different shapes.
Smothering shadows strangle and choke the sky.
The damp slithers and slides, slips and curls round the chimney pot.
Looking for his victim, blurring and blinding the distant view.
Floating, sweeping along the grass.
In the distance I hear a muffled voice calling to a friend.

Deborah Blanchett, 8 yrs.

In this piece, Deborah puts her extensive vocabulary to good use. She employs the techniques of alliteration: 'Smothering shadows strangle...', '...blurring and blinding...' and assonance (the repetition of vowel sounds) as in 'Tickling the cobwebs as it trickles...'. Deborah is now close to the next stage in her development as a writer when she will need to trim down and select words

Deborah has chosen to write her poem using long lines which well match the lumbering movements of the large animal to which the fog is compared. Later the animal changes shape but it is still nasty, still 'looking for a victim.'

The last line brings a human touch to the poem.

● **THE DRAGONS INSIDE ME**

– – – – – – – – – – – – – – – – – – –

The dragons inside of us are all the different thoughts and feelings we have – greed, anger, hate, hunger, meanness, joy, jealousy. What do these dragons look like, move like, sound like and what do they do? To simplify the presentation of this poem each idea starts with the repetitive phrase 'There is a – dragon inside of me'. List all the thoughts and feelings that the class can think of and ask them to write one dragon idea for each – about six or seven will make a good sized piece.

●   *The Dragons Inside Me*

There is a soft dragon inside me
that makes me hand out comfort.

There is a nosy dragon inside me
that stretches my nose into trouble.

There is a sleepy dragon inside me
that forces me up to bed too early.

There is a curious dragon inside me
that makes me peep through rusty keyholes.

There is a fierce dragon inside me
that makes me slam doors.

There is a hungry dragon inside me
that has licked my head clean of ideas.

Lindsay Iles, 10 yrs.

The idea comes from Carl Sandburg's poem *'Wilderness'* (part of which is reproduced below), in which he writes of all the animals that might be trapped inside the wilderness of the body.

●   **Wilderness**

There is a wolf in me ... fangs pointed for tearing gashes ... a red tongue for raw meat ... and the hot lapping of blood – I keep this wolf because the wilderness gave it to me and the wilderness will not let it go.

There is a hog in me ... a snout and a belly ... a machinery for eating and grunting ... a machinery for sleeping satisfied in the sun – I got this too from the wilderness and the wilderness will not let it go.

There is a fish in me ... I know I came from salt-blue water-gates ... I scurried with shoals of herring ... I blew waterspouts with porpoises ... before land was ... before the water went down ... before Noah ... before the first chapter of Genesis.

O, I got a zoo, I got a menagerie, inside my ribs, under my bony head, under my red-valve heart – and I got something else: it is a man-child heart, a woman-child heart: it is a father and mother and lover: it came from God-Knows-

Where: it is going to God-Knows-Where – For I am the
keeper of the zoo: I say yes and no: I sing and kill and
work: I am a pal of the world. I came from the wilderness.

Carl Sandburg

● ***There is a Pig ...***

There is a pig inside me
snorting through his food.
There is a dog inside me
that barks at everyone.
There is a cat inside me
that scratches everyone in sight.
There is a page inside me
that rustles all the time.
There is a name inside me
that calls 'Peter'.
There is a crow
inside me that flies
all around my heart.
There is a fish inside
of me that swims around
in my blood.
There is a boy inside me
that shouts and screams.
There is a nest inside me
that tickles my tummy.
There is a desk inside me
that keeps all my ideas.

Emavel Rodriguez, 8 yrs.

● **HANDS**

- -

What somebody's hands look like seems to say so much
about them. Ask the class to draw carefully round the outline
of their hands and then copy in the shape of their nails, the
predominant lines and wrinkles. Can they count the number
of bones in their hands by feeling? Using an ink pad take
finger prints. Inspect and copy the patterns down. Draw the
main lines on the palm of your hand. Using square graph
paper calculate the area of your hand by drawing its outline

and adding up the cm squares. Find out how much your hand can pick up by using marbles or dried beans. . . . There are many activities to do with hands that we can use to encourage the class to look and think about how valuable they are to us.

When it comes to writing, I would ask the class to look closely at every line, wrinkle, lump and bump. Start with the back of the hand, the knuckles, the fist, fingers, nails, tips, pads, the palm and wrist. Think about some of the things hands are used for, many of them opposing each other – giving/taking, helping/hurting, building/destroying.

If hands has become a mini topic, you could give everyone a piece of sugar paper and ask them to produce a large wall poster using drawings, graphs, information and writing. This would, of course, depend on the class and your judgement of them.

● **My Thumb**

My thumb is like a shrunken finger that has been made fatter.
A huge electronic fly crusher.
A fat button pusher.
A thing to stick in your mouth.
A sign to say okay.
A model for finger puppets.
An enormous scaly monster.

Kerry Colbran, 8 yrs.

● *My Hand*

My hand curls up.
My knuckles swell,
    like a football being pumped up.
My fist clenches.
Ready to collect my revenge.
My fingers bow to the king.
The smallest of them all.
The king is the thumb.

Mark Sheppard, 8 yrs.

● **Hands**

My hands are like spiders discovering
new objects.
They fidget about from place to place
It curls up into a large ball ready to stun
the thing which approaches.

the knuckles are like hills as hard as stone.
My fingers are like daggers which grip and
claw and pinch the crevices, are smothered
in hairs the lines creep over my palm
and close sharply when my fist closes up
once again and spider rests.

Richard Cobbold, 10 yrs.

● **CATS**

- -

The double life of a cat make a fascinating contrast. In the day-time they are soft, purring, sleepy creatures, but at night they become savage, sly hunters. Discussion should contrast this double-edged life. Avoid such words as 'nice', 'lovely' and concentrate on thinking about how a cat really behaves.

The poem 'Eight ways of touching' is 8 verses long. Each verse has 14 words in it and is seven lines long. This is a challenging new form for children to try and adapt. It was invented by the poet George MacBeth.

● **Powerful Sugar**

His mouth strains open once again.
He heaves himself up and
half opens his eyes. The greenness
sparkles wildly in his eye.
He prowls around my dustbin
and licks the kit-e-kat tin.
He spots a tasty morsel.
He crouches low and pounces.
He has caught his morsel.
He hits it from paw to paw,
claws stabbing his throat.
He grips the mouse in the
jagged teeth. Sugar is proud
of himself and rips the mouse
and chews it.

Richard Cobbold, 10 yrs.

● **Good Night Sugar**

His luminous eyes glint
in the darkness of the

evening.
His sleek slender tail sways
in the bitter breeze. He winks
lovingly at me. He arches his
back and kneads on the dew wet
grass. His mouth strains open,
his jagged teeth embedded in his jaw.
The roof of his mouth is crinkled
and you can see his cold
elegant bones arching his jaw.

Richard Cobbold, 10 yrs.

Eight ways of touching my cat Sugar

You can pat
his spine
and see his sleek
slender
tail
arise up
high.

You can blow
in his
ear and he will
twitch
and bend
his
legs.

You can tickle
his tummy
and he will bite
and
show
his huge
jaws.

You can pull
a string
along the floor
and
see
him
pounce on it.

You can stroke
his chin
and he will purr
wildly
and
screw his
eyes.

You can pull his
tail
and see him leap
into
the
thin absorbent
air.

You can pull
his leg
and watch him
stumble
like
an
old hobbled
woman.

You can stare
him in
the eye and he
will
wink
suspiciously at
you.

Richard Cobbold, 10 yrs.

These three poems were about Richard's own cat.

All too often poems about cats simply descend into a description of a cat catching a mouse and killing it. The poem becomes a story in which the cat spots a victim, stalks it, pounces and then eats it. Although many of us have witnessed the fruits of a cat's hunting delivered to our doors, few young writers will have closely observed a cat in action. Therefore, what is written about can rapidly become dishonest.

● **THIS MORNING...**

- -

When your class are used to writing – can think quickly, have built up a wide vocabulary and are used to coming up with original ideas, play this game with them. Everyone writes a sentence at a time with the teacher giving instructions as to what each sentence should be about. The class only have one minute per sentence, then everyone moves on to the next. Each sentence begins with the words 'This morning...' and the children have to add what happened. Here are some suggestions for what each sentence might be about.

1   *A lie.*
2   *Something to do with a noise.*
3   *Something to do with an object.*
4   *Something to do with a number.*
5   *Something to do with a colour.*
6   *Something to do with a character from a book.*
7   *Something to do with an animal.*
8   *Something to do with an emotion.*
9   *Something to do with the Past, Present or Future.*

The tenth line should round off the poem. This idea could be adapted in many ways and it is surprising how good the results can be for such a brief period of time.

● This Morning...

This Morning I came to school on a bone dry tongue.
This Morning a book cracked open and the words fell out.
This Morning number 5 was stung by a hive.
This morning the colour red was dreaming upside down in his bed.
This Morning C.S. Lewis knocked on my door to see Aslan.
This Morning a baboon popped a balloon.
This Morning sorrow giggled.

**This Morning the past came as a flame and I wrung it's neck.
In the evening I called the Morning to me and sliced it to
shreds.**

Timothy Clapham, 8yrs.

●   **SUN**

- -

There are a considerable number of words to do with the sun,
how it shines and its effects on the ground, plants, animals,
the road surface and us. What does it feel like? Where would
you like to be when it is blazing down? What do people do in
the hot weather – what do you see, hear, (ice-cream van,
children playing), taste, smell?

If it is not a sunny day try to recreate the atmosphere through
your discussion. When they write, ask them to imagine what
it is like on a hot day, hold that picture in their minds and
describe it. The poems can be copied onto brightly coloured
suns that could hang as mobile poems.

The Sun

Boiling,
Burning,
Like a furnace,
Gas Flames,
Stretching out like the
fingers of Lucifer,
Blistering,
Blazing,
A deadly fireball,
An evil star,
But it gives us
light and life,
It is like a
lightbulb in the sky,
A piece of burning coal,
In a fireplace of planets
and stars,
A golden speck in the
universe,
A copper coin in the sky,
In a money-box of silver stars.

Adrian Morris, 10 yrs.

The Sun Rise

*A bright sun gleaming in the
window
The glass shimmers
on
the red and
blue sky
The shadows of
The sun
lay
stretched on
The path
like butterflies wings
The red
flames
are like
rubies
They split in half
The sun
is made of
spitting
hot glass.*

Amanda Cornwell, 8 yrs.

● **WHO DO YOU THINK YOU ARE?**

— —

This is a chance to be funny in an indignant way. The poem is in couplets the first line always being

'Who do you think you are...'

and the second line being the suggestion of something very naughty...

'putting glue into my shoes?'

Remind the class to try to think of new ideas of their own, read out the examples and let them make some up. Remind them that each question ends with a question mark. A popular way to round off the lesson is by hearing some read aloud.

● **Who do you think you are?**

Who do you think you are,
cutting the table in half?

Who do you think you are
having a bath in my bed,
cutting the telephone line,
cuddling a snake?

Who do you think you are,
putting ice-cubes down my welly boots,
giving the teachers a thousand lines,
tying my cat's tail against the kettle?

Who do you think you are,
chopping my ruler into bits and eating it,
pushing me off the roof of a multi-storey block of flats,
tying my laces together so that I fall over?

Who do you think you are,
shooting peas at old ladies,
throwing my brother's contact lenses into the river,
pouring porridge on my chair?

Who do you think you are,
putting ferrets down my trousers?
Who do YOU think you are...?

Group Poem

_ _

Most children eventually come across the famous wardrobe which Lucy steps through in *'The Lion, The Witch and The Wardrobe'* to enter another world. If you found a secret door, what might lie on the other side? Ask your class to look through their magic doors and invent the craziest dream worlds they can imagine.

This sort of idea is particularly useful when teaching a class with a mixed age group. So Matthew, a fourth year, writes,

> *I ran through the secret door and saw the crystal of youth. It gleamed in the sun.*

> *I walked through the magic door and saw 3 miniature men digging for happy dreams.*

Whilst Joanna, who is a second year, writes,

> *I ran through the magic door and saw a gold kettle.*

By gluing two pieces of paper together and cutting a door in the top piece you can make a display of doors that open to reveal the poems written inside.

● ***The Magic Door***

> I stepped through the secret door
> and saw an elephant who was waiting
> to take you to the Devil.

> I wandered through the magic door
> and saw a remarkable lion
> who had wings.

> I ran through the secret door
> and saw a dragon that lived on the sun.

> I was pushed through the magic door
> and saw mirrors that made you fat and thin.

> I walked through the secret door
> and saw God putting the moon in the sky.

> Abbey Dougall, 8 yrs.

—————————————————————

What is the pool like before you jump in? As you enter the water how does it feel?
Collect words to describe moving through water, being under water, how the water behaves and what it feels like to swim (or flounder).

The piece of writing can have a unity if children describe their feelings before, during and after the swim. This is an ideal lesson to follow the first swim of the year.

● *Swimming*

A clear sheet of glass unshaken,
*   a moment's hesitation then*
*   I dive,*

Shattering the mirror,
*   The water stings my arms and*
*   legs, freezing my body,*

The water engulfs me like a fish into
*   its belly,*

Now I am a glittering fish,
*   My scales shimmering as I*
*   glide through the icy*
*   cold depths of the pool,*

Consuming the air greedily,
*   I come up gasping,*
*   like a fish,*

I disappear again,
*   Completely stunned,*

I crash to the bottom,
*   My eyes stinging,*
*   I grasp at the air*
*   But there's nothing*
*   there,*

My lungs are bursting,
*   My lips sealed,*
*   I grope around,*

My lips burst open,
*   The water cascades,*
*   Into my mouth,*

I regain myself,
*   I spurt upwards,*
*   Exploding through the*
*   Surface,*
*   Once again shattering it,*

I gasp at the air with
*   shock,*
*   I clamber out sitting on*
*   the side of the pool,*
*   Trembling,*
*   Shivering,*
*   and shaken.*

Kathryn Hoblin, 10 yrs.

● I WANT TO PAINT

This idea comes from a poem by Adrian Henri. It is a chance to create anything you like – the idea is that you could paint anything – a sound, a smell, a taste, a feeling, a thought, something impossibly large ... anything. Each idea is linked by the repetitive phrase 'I want to paint'. Read out the examples and ask the class to try their own. Point out that you only want their ideas, nothing like the ones you've read out, and that they can be as crazy and strange as they like.

● I Want To Paint...

I want to paint...

        pictures of England in every detail with
        everyone included,
        a microscopic bug as big as an elephant
        the most beautiful person ever born and the ugliest.

I want to paint...

        pictures of money and take some out now and
        again to spend,
        pictures of a beautiful world that I could have
        to myself and only let friends in.

I want to paint...

        black holes that twist and turn into nothing,
        the destruction of the earth and people
        floating in deep space,
        ships which haven't yet been designed,
        sadness walking streets, happiness dancing
        about on roofs.

I want to paint...

        elephants with every crease and wrinkle,
        every detail of an old man's bald head and
        bushy eyebrows.

I want to paint...

        the Queen saying a speech and most of the M.P.s
        leaning on their umbrellas,
        Denis Healey going to an eyebrow cut,
        Ronald Reagan going to sleep at one of his
        peace-making conferences.

I want to paint...

        big black spiders in my teacher's hair,
        cats walking along washing lines,
        ghosts from beyond a million galaxies,
        sunsets that make the earth cry.

I want to paint...

        every shade of blue in my left eye,
        all the freckles on my face in detail and
        in the right place,
        every stitch perfectly that's in my red jumper.

I want to paint...

        pictures that make the Hulk scream.

        Group Poem by 4th year Writers' Workshop

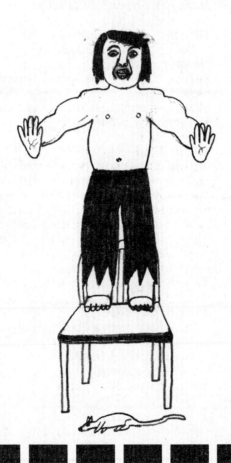

One • **A Small Dragon**
Read the Brian Patten poem *'A Small Dragon'*
in Penguin Modern Poets 10. Then discover
your own small dragon. Where? What does it
eat? What happens? Does anyone believe
you?

• *I walk by the cliff to see my friend the dragon.*
• *He lives in the rock.*
• *Some people would call him a fossil but I*
don't.
• *He has a curly tail and a long snout.*
• *I feed him on sea moss that grows nearby.*

Two • **Silence**
Silence ... *only the sharpening of a cat's*
claws against wood.
Silence ... *only the snap of a flower being*
picked.
• Silence ... *only the vibration of a loose*
exhaust on a rattling car.

Three • **A Cup of Tea**
Instead of the usual 'How to make a cup of tea'
or 'how to make a telephone call' – describe
the process by means of a poem with plenty
of interesting, colourful words and phrases.
• *... the hot hiss as the kettle whistles,*
• *the gurgling, snapping, whistling sound as I*
pour.
• *I look into the fat little pot*
And all my thoughts fizz fiercely to my head.

Four • **It could have been**
It could have been a dog howling in the
distance.
• *It could have been a bag moved by the breeze.*
• *It could have been ...*
• *But no it was only ....*

Five	**Sorry**
•	An extension of the idea in the poem *'This is just to say...'* by William Carlos Williams.
•	*Sorry lion for pinching your fur but I was cold.*
•	*Sorry bird for taking your wings but I wanted to fly...*

Six	**Shape poems**
•	Draw the outline of a cat and then write a poem about the cat within the framework.
•	Then erase the lines and the cat's shape should still be seen in the layout of the words.
•	Many ideas for shape poems – houses, stars, moon, ships.

Seven	**Laughter**
•	Think of as many ways as you can for defining laughter.
•	*Laughter like a soft wriggling worm.* *Laughter like a car staggering its engine.* *Laughter like a golden leaf falling down. etc.*

Eight	**I never saw**
•	*I never saw a palm tree but I know what its like to climb one in a hurricane.*
•	*I never saw a dinosaur but I know what its like to be held between the teeth of Tyrannosaurus.*

Nine	**The ghost in my head**
•	*There's a ghost in my head, he flies around when lights go out and bright yellow circles come twirling from my eyes.......*
•	Think about what we are really frightened of, and how it springs from within us, the product of our own fantasies.

Ten	**Why me?**
•	A chance to complain.
•	*Why is it me who does all the work and in return gets all the nagging?*
•	*Why is it me who runs the errands while my brother sits with his feet up watching T.V.*

● IF MY THOUGHTS TOOK SHAPE

Tell children to think of the cartoon characters they find in comics, whose thoughts are presented in picture form in speech bubbles. Then imagine how our thoughts would be pictured if they were captured in this way. Start by listing some different kinds of thoughts that we all have – angry thoughts, selfish, lazy, evil, sad, etc. Then try to think of what these thoughts remind you e.g. for anger, perhaps a lion or a charging bull.

● If My Thoughts Took Shape

If my evil thoughts took shape
they would be like a bully beating up
a defenceless child.

If my confusing thoughts took shape
they would be like roads leading
nowhere.

If my frightening thoughts took shape
they would be like a group of poisonous scorpions
all around me.

If my noisy thoughts took shape
they would be like an echoing band
in an empty room.

If my romantic thoughts took shape
they would be like the moon
reflecting on a lake.

If my quiet thoughts took shape
they would be like leaves
rippling gently on a canal.

If my imaginative thoughts took shape
they would be like a flower
going shopping.

If my furious thoughts took shape
they would be like a
stormy night at sea.

If my lazy thoughts took shape
they would be like someone
slouching in a chair.

If my selfish thoughts took shape
I wouldn't tell anyone
in the whole world.

Group Poem

If possible visit a place where gargoyles may be examined
e.g. a church or castle (or cemetery for stone figures). What
purpose do gargoyles serve? What are they looking at? What
have they seen? You might like to imagine that they speak to
each other at night and then try to write a conversation
between two gargoyles. Alternatively, write down a
gargoyle's thoughts in the form of a poem.

How do they feel about people pointing and making hurtful
remarks.

What does time do to stone faces?

In the pieces that follow, note the assonance in Lindsay's
poem (intentional or otherwise), where words with the same
vowel sounds – years, here, peering – help to strengthen the
rhythm and flow of the piece. Note too, the double echo of
two words at the end of John Flann's poem – 'weather eaten/
beaten'. We expect to see 'beaten' and are surprised to find
'eaten', but how effective it is.

Angel Faces

We will wait for years
to crumble into dust.
Children come and go
But we remain.
We stand like spies
Hidden in our cover of grimy moss
As silent as the air.
We are like stars
Staring down at the earth.
We are left to crumble, wither,
Like a plant without water.
We are blind as moles
and deaf as the sky.
We are only stone.

Debbie Osman, 10 yrs.

Whose Angel Are You?

Whose angel are you?
Your arms are cracked,
Your body is tangled
With lichen and moss.

Whose angel are you?
Suffering erosion
With invincible strength
Gazing at the crop of dead bodies.

Angel, your time is up.
Your body is no more.
The person who carved you died,
He made your eyes blind
And made your wings out of stone, like
A tree rooted
To the ground.

Solid and cold
Your form is paralyzed
By the frozen leves
Tangled and weather eaten.

John Flann, 10 yrs.

- *Gargoyle*

With hideous head and glaring eyes
I was made to stare down upon all.
For years I have sat up here
Peering with my beady eyes way down on the town.
For years I have feared that
I should crumble and fall
hundreds of feet to the ground.
I have prayed that once I should walk
among the glamorous people,
but never was my prayer answered.
I stare into the beautiful glass window,
through the rows of polished pews.
I wish to sit there but no.
Of all the grotesque monsters
I am the worst.
I am the GARGOYLE.

Lindsay Iles, 10 yrs.

- **WHAT YOU ARE**

This is an idea from a poem by Roger McGough found in
Penguin Modern Poets 10 *'The Mersey Sound'*. It is a series of
extended metaphors describing someone in terms of

something else. The 'someone' may be a fictional creation or based firmly in a real person.

The idea is to sum up someone's character, bearing in mind that no one is entirely black or white. Most people are full of contradictions. Perhaps one day – 'the rushing river swelling with anger', while another day, 'the flutter of a moth's wings round a candle flame'.

As well as from day to day, someone may be seen as being one thing at midnight but quite another at midday.

> You are the din of a punk rock band at midnight,
> You are the blood coloured sun scorching the daylight.

McGough in his poem makes use of other techniques and these could also be explored:

> You are the distance between...
> You are the moment when...

Also consider 'What he is...' poems or 'What she is...'

● **What You Are** *(Extracts)*

**you are the cat's paw
among the silence of midnight goldfish**

**you are the waves
which cover my feet like cold eiderdowns**

**you are the teddybear (as good as new)
found beside a road accident**

**......
you are the blind mirror
before the curtains are drawn back**

**you are the drop of dew on a petal
before the clouds weep blood**

**you are the sweetfresh grass that goes sour
and rots beneath children's feet**

**......
you are the distance
between the accident and the telephone box
measured in heartbeats**

**......
you are the moment
before the noose clenched its fist
and the innocent man cried: treason**

Roger McGough

What you are

You are the moon drifting
Through the cold air of a winter's night.
You are the eye of an owl's face
Shining in the misty dark sky.
You are the dew in the jungle
Settling on the big leaves.
You are the tongue of a great
grizzly bear.
You are the toe nails of a
fox going silently over the
silver moon.
You are the mist caught on some
barb-wire screaming for its life.
You are the Jack frost flying
over the sky dropping snow.
You are the Arch-way
standing still over steps.
You are the name of a book
drifting through space.
You are the life of a little baby,
idle and helpless.

Hayley Kemp, 8 yrs.

She Is

She is like a golden star,
slinking into the night.
She is like a flower of light.
She is like a silent pair of lips saying
something unknown.
She is like a brilliant spurt of love.
She is like an ungrateful silence.

Matthew Cole, 7 yrs.

What You Are

You are the sly dog
waiting outside the rabbit's burrow.

You are the distance between
the light of night, the darkness of day.

You are the scream of the car
as it blinks at death.

You are the moment when the trap-door
opens and a scream goes up.

You are the 'suddenly'
when something terrible happens.

Barry Harvey, 11 yrs.

He is

He is in a misty cloud that floats through a bewildered sky.
He is in swirling smoke that bows at his honour.
He is in a sharp flash of fierce lightning.
He is the sharp blade of a golden knife.
He is a buzzing fly that shimmers in a velvet web.

Timothy Clapham, 8 yrs.

Tonight at Noon is about reversing normality. The idea stems from a poem by Adrian Henri in Penguin Modern Poets 10, *'The Mersey Sound'*.

Tonight at noon
Supermarkets will advertise 3d EXTRA on everything
Tonight at noon
Children from happy families will be sent to live in a home.
Elephants will tell each other human jokes
America will declare peace on Russia
World War I generals will sell poppies in the streets
    on November 11th
The first daffodils of autumn will appear
When the leaves fall upwards to the trees

Tonight at noon
Pigeons will hunt cats through city backyards
Hitler will tell us to fight on the beaches and on the
    landing fields
A tunnel full of water will be built under Liverpool
Pigs will be seen flying in formation over Woolton
and Nelson will not only get his eye back but his arm as well
White Americans will demonstrate for equal rights
in front of the Black House
and the monster has just created Dr. Frankenstein

Girls in bikinis are moonbathing
Folksongs are being sung by real folk
Artgalleries are closed to people over 21
Poets get their poems in the Top 20
Politicians are elected to insane asylums
There's jobs for everyone and nobody wants them
In back alleys everywhere teenage lovers are kissing
in broad daylight
In forgotten graveyards everywhere the dead will quietly
bury the living
and
You will tell me you love me
Tonight at noon

        Adrian Henri

Children love the idea of a 'topsy-turvy' world where it is adults who get spanked and sent to bed, where cars drive themselves or where elephants tell human jokes!

With this idea, children are able to move away from concrete descriptions towards playing with words. Good ideas now become very important. It is easy to be silly with this and much more difficult to come up with really clever and amusing ideas.

● **Tonight at Noon**

Tonight at noon, humans will suck blood from vampires.
Adults will get a good hiding and be sent up to bed with no
                                                        supper.
Burglars will ring the bell and ask if they can steal the silver.
Mice will be scared of elephants.
Tonight at noon, rats will swoop down and kill owls,
Humans will pinch crabs' toes,
Electric eels will get a nasty shock.
Night torches will find their way through sun-filled caves.
Tower bridge will fall up.
Tonight at noon, humans will infect diseases,
Cars will drive people,
And when you meet me we will say goodbye,
Tonight at noon.

Barry Harvey, 11 yrs.

● **ACROSTICS**

– –

An acrostic is a poem where the first letter of each line spells a word. Thus the first line of the poem begins with the first letter of the word, the second line with the second letter and so on until all the letters of the word have lines to themselves.

This technique means that children have to think harder about the way they say something.

The acrostic slows down the hasty child as the poem must still read well, and it is thus necessary to choose both the best words and the best sentence construction within the limitations imposed by the form.

A start can be made with animal acrostics, including such mythical creatures as DRAGON, UNICORN, PHOENIX, GRIFFIN, etc.

It may be necessary to impose a lower limit of letters as some children will immediately see the benefits to be gained from tackling animals with 3-letter names – CAT, DOG, ANT!

A ctively springing through the bushes
N arrow legs move with speed and rhythm
T ender eyes look with sorrow across the open pampas
E mbroidering the ground with tracks in a wild pattern
L azily he lowers his delicate head to the water
O pen caves beckon him to the cliffs and shelter
P oisonous snakes rise up to bite him but he kicks them away
E legant creature of the jungle, wary of every danger.

Helen Menzies-Sacher, 10 yrs.

C hasing his prey with great ambition,
H auling his catch out of sight.
E ating savagely
E xploding with a war of anger when
T he mischievous hyenas stole
A leg of his catch
H e warns them off with a tremendous challenge.

Mark Milford, 10 yrs.

● **I STOOD IN A ROOM FULL OF...** _ _ _ _ _ _ _ _

This idea is written in couplets where the second line expands on the image expressed in the first.

Tell the class to imagine themselves standing in a room filled with whatever they like. Then, in the second line, they must either say what happens to them, or what happens to the room.

e.g. *I stood in a room full of darkness*
and my eyes pulled down their blinds.

I stood in a room full of fizzy drinks
and the room exploded.

A composite poem may be put together from the best lines of individual children.

I stood in a room full of monsters
and I started to roar.

I stood in a room full of confusion
and my head burst.

I stood in a room full of clouds
and the thoughts scurried across my mind.

I stood in a room full of prayers
and shouted 'Oh Father'.

I stood in a room full of ghosts
and the spirits wandered through me.

I stood in a room full of snakes
and I started to twist and turn.

I stood in a room full of riot
and it made my eardrums pound.

I stood in a room full of adults
and I grew and GREW and GREW.

I stood in a room full of emptiness
and I became hollow.

I stood in a room full of alligators
and I snapped at my Mum when she spoke to me.

I stood in a room full of faces
and I couldn't find my own.

Group Poem

● **KITE**

- -

There must be few children who haven't flown some sort of kite at one time or another. Kites come in many shapes, sizes and designs, from the simple diamond to the fiery Chinese dragon. Make a large collection of words to describe the movements of the kite – how it twists and turns, loops and dives according to the will of the wind. Describe how you control the kite, despite the wind's efforts to tear it from you.

The finished pieces could be written out and stuck onto kite shapes. These could then be made into mobiles.

● **The Kite**

A small boy stands on the sands, gazing upwards,
tightly holding on to the tugging strings.
The kite sweeps over watching waters below,
diving, gliding, looping, soaring gracefully –
doing tricks that the beaming-faced boy leads it into.

The gaily-coloured kite proudly soars and dips, soars
and dips into the motionless waters.
The boy on the beach pulls on the strings ...
dreaming himself as a world champion
him and his KITE!

Kerry Dale, 11 yrs.

● ### *Kite*

Enormous wings glide on the wind,
Sweeping in and out of imaginary hoops,
The kite races through the sky,
Struggling to get free,
But a boy grips on the handle,
Banning its freedom.
It dives and dips,
And then swiftly moves up into the clouds,
the boy glows with happiness
and thinks only of his graceful kite
In the deep sky.

Ainne Dennison, 11 yrs.

In these poems something extra is evident. The movement
and actions of the kites are well described but there is also a
new depth to the writing which comments on the description.
This is shown well in lines such as 'banning its freedom' from
Ainne's piece.

● ## ARE YOU AN OBSERVER?

– –

This lesson can be done inside and outside. Remind your
class to use their 5 senses and to look closely at the subject
they are writing about for details.

Either hand out a selection of previously gathered objects –
such as, an old clock, leather shoe, camera, candle, belt,
ornate mug, a battered hat, jewel box, brooch etc. . . . or take
them outside and ask them to select something they can see
to write about . . . a tree, the school railings, a flower tub,
windows, chimneys. They will need to focus carefully on
details so ask them to draw the object first and then write
about it.

The Phone

Hard, black and shiny
Waiting silently,
For you to dial slowly and steadily.
As you put the reciever to your ear
It gently purrs like a cat
washing itself.

Claire Baldwin, 9 yrs.

The Compass

Its slick silver slit legs
slither apart.
A ballet-dancer
accomplishes the splits.

Kyron Brabon, 10 yrs.

The Top Of The Gate

The silent black metal,
a twist of curving materials.
The bats delicate wings are stiff
as if they knew they were dead.
An antenni towers at the top,
catching the glittering sun.
Trains of moss have slithered up the gleaming structure.
I wonder how many children have staggered underneath.

Simon Overbury

Poem

Skeleton leaf
lifeless like tissue
laces neatly threaded
gentle, fragile
the silk delicate embroidery
the veins spreading
network carefully stitched
boney like witch's
fingers
backbone gentle and
tender

Sally Crone, 9 yrs.

IN MY HEAD

— — — — — — — — — — — — — — — — —

This idea stemmed from the poem by Czech poet Miroslav
Holub 'A Boy's Head' and from a follow-up art lesson where
children drew round the silhouettes of their heads and then

tried to show in an amusing way, how the different parts functioned. The brain was drawn as a library of books, or a computer, or a clockwork motor, while a tape recorder served as a memory bank. As the picture grew more complicated it seemed a good exercise to try to describe the ideas in words to complement and clarify the pictorial approach.

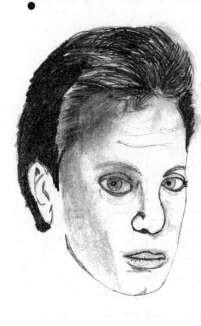

A Boy's Head

In it there is a space-ship
and a project
for doing away with piano lessons.

And there is
Noah's ark,
which shall be first.

And there is
an entirely new bird,
an entirely new hare,
an entirely new bumble-bee.

There is a river
that flows upwards.

There is a multiplication table.

There is anti-matter.

And it just cannot be trimmed.

I believe
that only what cannot be trimmed
is a head.

There is much promise
in the circumstance
that so many people have heads.

Miroslav Holub

In My Head

In my head there is a trapped wasp buzzing to get out.
In my head there's an exploding volcano gushing anger.
In my head there's a plastic bag containing all the ideas I can't find
In my head there's a helicopter blowing air out of my ears.
In my head there's a man with a hosepipe putting water on my eyes and
                                                        making me cry.
In my head there's a clockwork brain which the manager winds up.
In my head there's a bunch of keys but only one of them fits into the lock.
In my head there's a microphone which picks up the slightest noise.
In my head there is a red devil who points to who I hate.
In my head there is a hammer thumping out the rhythm of my headache.
In my head there's a bath to clean my bad thoughts and a sponge to
                                    scrub off the scars in my memory bank.

In my head there's a crystal ball to show me my future.
In my head there's a plan, a plan to escape to Venus.
In my head there's a little man by my eyes who drives me but sometimes
he falls asleep & **I CRASH.**

Group Poem

● **HAIKUS**

– –

A haiku is a traditional Japanese form of poetry containing seventeen syllables. It is usually illustrated.

Begin by telling the class that you want them to write you a 3-lined poem. Their reactions will probably be on the lines of, "Is that all?" Then point out some of the problems your class will face in trying to get those 3 lines correct. The basic one will be in sticking to the pattern of five syllables in the first line, seven in the second, and five in the third. (A syllables test may be useful here.)

Point out to the class that haikus are essentially 'word snapshots' where each word used has to 'pull its weight' and that many haikus are about aspects of nature and landscape.

To write a good haiku is a difficult task but children should persevere with the 5–7–5 pattern. It is an excellent exercise in word choice and in working away at an idea until it can be expressed in the correct form.

I suggest that at first the following pattern could be used.

1st line . . . . . **time of day**
2nd line . . . . **focus on something**
3rd line . . . . . **compare it to something else**

e.g. *Cold frosty sunrise* **5**
Telegraph poles stand lonely **7**
like the masts of ships **5**

When a reasonable result has been achieved, have it copied out in very best handwriting. Encourage children to think carefully about where the haiku should be placed on the page. Then illustrate with pen and ink.

Other examples:

A hot summer noon,
Ice cubes tingle in cold drinks
Like soft harness bells.

Kerry Dale, 11 yrs.

The quiet evening,
No noise from the lonely streets;
A distant owl hoots.

Karla Grayling, 11 yrs.

Icicles stab the air,
The frost closes its jaws,
Icy wind attacks.

Adrian Morris, 10 yrs.

A winter morning.
Grey fog creeping the cold earth;
A grey dufflecoat.

Kathryn Hoblin, 10 yrs.

After haiku, other forms could be attempted. The Japanese *'tanka'* has five lines in a pattern of 5,7,5,7,7 syllables. Again, as with haiku, tankas are word pictures. Children may find it difficult to stick rigidly to the syllable pattern and a little leeway should be allowed at the teacher's discretion.

● **Trees**

Brown arms are waving,
Gently shaking their foliage.
Continuous movement
Cutting passages through air,
And fighting the growing wind.

Children may also enjoy writing cinquains – another short form with strict limitations on words or syllables. These five line poems with a 2,4,6,8,2 syllable pattern are again best attempted after a lot of work with breaking down words.

Less able writers may prefer to tackle an adaptation of the strict form which follows a word pattern of 1,2,3,4,1 words per line. The first line should always be the name of the subject and the last a synonym or exclamation. The 2nd, 3rd and 4th lines should describe the subject in more detail, perhaps with a comment from the writer as in line four below:

Ginger-Ale
Refreshing, tasty,
Mouth-watering, gas-bubbling, breath-taking.
The best witches' potion.
Marvellous!

Rachel Smith, 10 yrs.

Considerable liberties may be taken with hyphenated words!

Further work may be attempted with writers who enjoy thinking about syllables. They can be encouraged to write longer pieces to a strict syllable pattern, perhaps with 10 syllables per line, or a 10,8,10,8 pattern. An effective rhythm can result when these poems are read aloud.

● **_Fishing Summer_**

Michael and I were fishing companions
rushing to catch the tide before it turned,
our tackle spilling from saddlebags, our
pockets crammed with fat paper wallets of
fresh dug lug. And casting we'd encounter
familiar hazards, reels span at our first
attempts, our lines tangled, sprouted birds' nests:
we spent precious time unravelling till
tides turned and fish bit fast. We caught an
old lag of a crab that came up fighting:
It bubbled and spat, with vicious claws splayed
out like a baseball catcher, then edged off
sideways across the pier to drop-plop down
to water beneath............

Brian Moses

Eventually children may reach a stage where you will wish to allow them to choose the form to be used for a particular piece of writing. Some will opt for repetition of a line with their own ideas tacked on, others will prefer a more open approach, while some children will attempt one of the strict forms outlined above. A discussion of form can only be done after a build up of vocabulary and after the children have had a lot of practice at the different forms.

When children become interested in counting syllables or words and inventing their own patterns, the content often suffers for a while, in a similar way to when they first start joining up their writing. For a while their main concern becomes the problem of counting the words or listening for the syllables. As they become more practiced at this they discover that they can use a pattern more easily and concentrate still on what they want to say.

Often the first few lines have a rhythm and regular syllable count of their own. They should use this to decide how the rest of the poem should flow. As a rough guide when writing, lines of a similar length will usually be of a similar syllable count ... it helps to keep re-reading the poem as it builds up. This way you can spot a clumsy line that does not fit the rhythm of the poem, you can 'hear if it sounds right'. John Betjeman describes his way of working:

'A line comes to me. It gives me the beginnings of the rhythm for the poem. I put down the line on the nearest available bit of paper – the back of a cigarette packet or a letter (which consequently doesn't get answered) and think about the rest of the poem in trains, driving a motor car, bicycling or walking – wherever I can be alone and recite the words out loud until they seem to be the right ones in the right order. I write very slowly and copy the completed draft out five or six times before I am contented with it.'

In 'Storm', Ramon counts his words, using a pattern of 2/4 repeated. The poem retains his compressed style and the word limitations add to this. Stripped to its bare bones the poem's language forcefully complements the power of the storm. In 'The Flame' Simon tries out using a syllable count for the first time, 4/7/4 syllables per verse. The poem reads well and he has attempted a mysterious image in the third verse.

Storm

The thunder
splits silence, shatters calm.
Sky rent,
wrenched into a muscular
explosion. Lightning
spears, veins slender and
slim spitting
acute to the ground.
Forked yellowy
threads spill, zig zagging
to earth.
Rain rages in fury,
beating, driving
its icy whips to
the window
panes, cascading down
in streams
of punches, ricocheting off
car boots.

Ramon Rodriguez, 10 yrs.

The Flame

The flame flickers,
burning brightly in the dark;
the wax drips down.

I stare at it,
seeing motionless shadows
on the candle.

The shadows stare,
eyeing my staring green eyes,
like a window.

A red spark fires,
with white wax burning slowly.
The candle sinks.

Simon Overbury, 9 yrs.

One
- **Clown**
  Play Ralph McTell's *'Clown'* or just talk about the dual personality of the clown. Think of the clown away from the laughter, away from the lights.

- *The Lifeless Clown*

  My handkerchief is saturated
  with white cloudy tears.
  Life is a hazard.
  i have no use for the wretched thing.

  Richard Tuff, 9 yrs.

Two
- **What I like about/What I hate about**
  What I like about rain is that it makes patterns on the windows.
- *What I hate about my sister is that she bosses me about.*

Three
- **The fire inside me – Anger**
  Try to describe what happens when you are angry. Think through the whole process from the birth of your angry feelings until the moment they subside. Are your feelings like a fire, a volcano, a tidal wave . . . ?

Four
- **If I**
  If I put on the suit of jealousy I would spit fire on my victims.
- *If I put on the cloak of greatness I would stand with power over everyone.*
- *If I put on the mask of cruelty I would whip people's minds.*

Five
- **Do not touch**
  How many of us are tempted to touch something when we know we shouldn't. What are the consequences if we do?
- *If I hadn't touched the black cat at midnight then I wouldn't have turned into a frog.*
- *If I hadn't touched my mum's cream cakes then I wouldn't have stomach ache.*
- *If I hadn't slid down the banisters etc . . .*

Six	**The Train**
•	Think of either watching a train or waiting for a train at night. How does the train look as it passes you?
•	*... Windows like bright yellow squares in rows, smearing into one another.*
•	What can you hear? Is it real or is it a mystery train?

Seven	**The Key**
•	*This is the key that kept my mind in motion.*
•	*This is the key that unlocked the secret of my hand.*
•	*This is the key ... etc.*

Eight	**Rules**
•	Ten rules for an art lesson.
•	Ten rules for going to sleep.
•	Ten rules for annoying your teacher

| e.g. | **1** *Always draw lines with a crooked ruler.*
2 *Always direct V.I.P.s to the boiler room.* |

Nine	**The empty house**
	Somehow it is always possible to tell when a house is empty. How do you feel on returning from school to discover no one at home, just an empty feeling that reaches out and pulls you inside?
•	*... I drop down into the cold chair* *and stare at the ceiling,* *then pull myself up and wander the room,* *impatient, agitated,* *and hope mum is back soon.*

Ten	**Wild Animal/Bird**
	Describe the creature very carefully – its body, how its moves, hunts etc. Make us see your subject – write about the surroundings, the time of day/year etc.

•	*Badger – Strolling along paths like a vicar*
	    on a Sunday walk.
	    Desolate cries echo throughout the
	    wood.
	    He
	      is
	        speaking.

● **WALLS**

Walls are built for two reasons:

a   *to keep something or someone inside them.*
b   *to keep something or someone outside them.*

Think of examples for each reason.

Point out how sometimes people build imaginary walls around themselves, perhaps to hide away from others.

Sometimes, too, people suffer through being on the outside of a wall almost carelessly thrown up by some other person or group.

Imaginary walls can hurt as much as real ones if you try to crash through them. Children readily understand this. They know all about the sudden appearances of 'walls' in the playground where one child is often isolated by the rest of his 'friendship' group. Discuss the phrase 'sent to Coventry'.

This is a sensitive area which can often result in some honest writing.

●   *The Walls*

Everywhere I look I can see huge walls.
My mind is filled
With the thought of walls.
My friends and my family are shouting
from the other side of the walls.
My body is forever touching hard, rough, unbearable bricks.
There is no warmth or comfort
Coming from the wall.
I shall stand on my feet and take each brick out one by one
and each brick shall count
as a step in my future.

                 Lynne Waller, 12 yrs.

●   **A Wall**

There is a wall between my family and me, a large wall they built brick by brick. I have got to get out but I can't, they are still building it.
How do I get out?
I suppose I built the wall, every yell another brick goes up. I kick the wall, glass appears on the top. Suddenly I stop to think. It all

started because I hit my brother. If I make up
with him, maybe the wall will disappear.
I sent a paper dart over the wall with just one
little word on it, 'Sorry'.
Slowly the wall disappears and we are friendly,
for a while.

Joanna Burgon, 9 yrs.

●   **MARBLING**

- -

Marbling is an easy and most effective method of producing
bright artwork. Coloured inks with an oil base are floated on
water. A sheet of paper is lowered onto the surface and picks
up a vivid print of the pattern that the inks have created. The
results are always different and never fail to excite and please
children. It was the combination of the strange shapes and
brilliant patterns that this art form can produce, mixed with
the children's excitement, that led us to think about writing
about marbling.

Every child needs to have made 2/3 prints for themselves.
They choose one to write about. The discussion that follows
should concentrate on

a   *the colours*
b   *the shapes they can see and what they remind*
          them of
c   *collecting words to describe the movement of*
          the patterns.

It is important for children to gain a sense of achievement
from their work – though marbling is, at its simplest level, a
trick of producing something that looks satisfying. It has,
however, never failed to stimulate the most exciting flow of
language.

The poems can be written straight onto the pattern or be
displayed beside it. Using a black felt tip pen and/or black
paper silhouettes, shapes can be outlined on the patterns.

●   *Colours*

Flowing colours swim across the page,
Spitting red, blue, orange, different colours

Wiggle lines across the paper,
Like fireworks exploding.
Into the black sky colours fly,
Everything is swirling, twirling into space.
Now in the sky I can see
Goats' eyes, birds' faces;
They swirl and curl, whirl around and around
Like clouds floating.
A snake's tail slithers across the page,
A jellyfish is there now
With the swirling colours everywhere
With spots of blood in the blue sky.
The whirlpool swirls red, orange, blue,
All the colours whizz and flicker,
The roots and veins twist and turn.
A crocodile swims in and out of the dancing colours;
I stretch the colours everywhere
So its head is long and its feet are stretching.
The hair in the wind blows freely;
The colours drift your dreams away.
Fish of all colours swim away and glide away.
A few spots of everything
And the red burns the paper.

Judy-Jane McGuire, 7 yrs.

Marbling

Swaying, swirling deep- sea ocean.
The curling multi-coloured lagoon,
the spitting fire of the dragon,
motionless mermaids,
    bubbling lava.
The slimy slow worms,
the golden genie,
    tangled up twisted streamers,
the squashed ocean blue.

Anne Winter, 11 yrs.

marbling

Mixtures of colours overlapping
mysterious faded, and weird shapes.
Whirling, flowing, mixing colours. Bubbles
and blobs, splurges spots joining and
swirling, whirling, circling and
twirling, curling into different colours.
Splashing flowing forming into colours an
pictures like waterfall, sea creature
weird faces, lava flowing, creating s

by

Kellie Parsons

Kellie Parsons, 11 yrs.

Kellie's poem is included because it effectively shows how
the 'swirling & curling' of the marbling can be suggested by
the pattern of her words as well as their meaning.

– – – – – – – – – – – – – – – – – – – –

Here we are encouraging children to come up with new, clever and often very funny ideas about their different features.

Refer back to 'Lies' poems written in the earlier stage and this time instead of accepting a straightforward lie e.g. my hands are made of matches, encourage the development of this idea so that the child can tell us what he does with his hands made of matches:

> *My hands are made of matches*
> *I strike people with them*
>
> *My nose is made of rubber*
> *it stretches into other people's business.*

Again, a good idea for composite poems.

●   **Myself**

My hands are like tractors digging up mud.
My fingers are like carrots so that when I bite my nails they crunch.
My mouth is like a black hole never coming to an end.
My hair is like a shaggy floor mop.
My tongue is a long pink pathway.
My blood is like a rushing river flowing to the sea.
My veins are like useless branches drooping down.
My head is like a machine carrying messages.
My bones ache and clatter when I move.
My ears are earphones listening.
My feet are like car tyres that skid and make a noise.
My hands are scuttling darting crabs running over the dark beach.
My heart is like a piston pumping and it will not stop pumping.

Group Poem

Children may produce images that do not seem to work – 'My veins are like useless branches drooping down'. From an adult's point of view this certainly seems inaccurate but a child's vision will often be different.

The first thing to decide is whether the image was forced for effect or whether it sprang spontaneously into the child's mind and was therefore a sincere part of that writer's vision. Images that have to be thought about or laboriously worked at usually do not succeed. The true image seems to arise from nowhere as a spontaneous connection that is quite magical.

Should we question an image that doesn't ring true? Certainly, images are to be treated with great respect for of all the things that we write down they are the most personal creations that we make; they are closest to us.

Perhaps here the writer was thinking of how the veins on her arms look like branches. It is the word 'useless' that seems inappropriate – after all, veins and branches are both useful in a similar way. It would be very off-putting to criticise every image a child suggests, even if for us it does not ring true.

When talking about images it is important to encourage those ideas that pop up from nowhere rather than ideas that have been over worked. Ask the class to write down, "What it reminds you of".

● **Ideas About Me**

My teeth are made of shutters,
they open and close all day.

My nose is made of rubber
and it stretches into other people's business.

My hair is made of rope,
it ties my skull together.

My fingers are made of people,
they try to control my body.

My toe-nails are made of balloons,
they take me to the stars.

My legs are made of jelly
and I wobble about on them.

My tears are made of mirrors
and they crack when my friends look in them.

My thumb is made of fire
It lights my candle at night.

My brain is made of spaghetti,
it tangles up the sums I work out.

My kidney is made of tambourines,
when I shake, it shakes with me.

My feet are two small wheat fields,
I grow corns on them.

My eyes are made of sapphires,
they blind people.

Group Poem

- -

In *'Tom's Midnight Garden'*, Tom discovers that when the Grandfather Clock strikes thirteen, a magical hour is created. Tom travels back in time to appear as a ghost. What else might happen in the magical 13th hour? A good way to start the children off is by reading some examples. Of course, this may well mean writing your own!

Warn the children about being too 'gory'. This is perhaps the moment to point out that through the understatement of an image, a magical, even sinister mood may be achieved.

Completed poems can be written carefully onto Grandfather Clock shapes which have moving pendulums fixed with brass paper fasteners. Alternatively you can make a small door which opens on the front of the clock where the pendulum usually swings. When the door is opened, the poem is revealed.

●   *The 13th Hour*

**In the 13th hour
the wind whispered
a secret into the
reed's roots.**

**In the 13th hour
the sun grew cold,
an icicle hung like
a tear.**

**In the 13th hour
the eyes of evil
twinkled with
happiness.**

**In the 13th hour
an egg broke its
heart of pure
gold.**

**In the 13th hour
lightning lost its
light and thunder
was struck dumb.**

**In the 13th hour
a claw stole the
soul of the earth.**

Timothy Clapham, 10 yrs.

●   *The 13th Hour*

In the thirteenth hour the stars disappeared and
the sky became a rumbling mass of cloud.
In the thirteenth hour grass stood stiff, erect
and electrified.
In the thirteenth hour paving stones
began to shift & overlap.
In the thirteenth hour insects began to swarm
together.

In the thirteenth hour the air went musty – food tasted strange.
In the thirteenth hour birds dropped from the trees.
In the thirteenth hour I saw a cat's eyeballs
expand & split his head open.
In the thirteenth hour eerie mutterings came over
the radio.
An eye watched from the T.V. screen which had
switched itself on. The kettle spout went rubbery
and reversed into the kettle.
In the thirteenth hour slaughtered birds hung
in a cold storeroom began to twitch, their hearts
began to beat, slowly, randomly.
In the thirteenth hour all colours reversed
completely, like a photographic negative.
In the thirteenth hour the carpet moved and wrapped
around someone, suffocating them.
In the thirteenth hour their skin peeled off
like damp wallpaper.
And long afterwards, their bones were still there,
to be examined by men, who shook their heads and waited –
for the thirteenth chime to strike again.
Mandy Crawford, 13 yrs.

● **BUS QUEUE**

– –

Children should be encouraged to write short clear descriptions so that the bus queue comes alive for the reader.

Discuss how someone's character and personality may be summed up in a few short lines which will ring true about that person.

Try to notice features of behaviour – stance, gestures, irritating habits etc. The way a person dresses can also tell us a lot.

● **Bus Queue**

A normal queue, just normal people except for that daft-looking teenager at the back. Long, round ear-rings danging down to her shoulders, lipstick covering all round her lips. Look at the man in front of her – stiff white colour, dented bowler hat. I can't see his face because it's stuck in a newspaper. Ah, look at that little girl holding her mother's hand, candyfloss smothering her mouth and a tatty-looking

*teddy under her arm. Her mother looks interesting – five
pound note sticking out of her pocket, a bag full of shopping
under her arm and a mouthful of something. Behind her a posh-
looking business man with an umbrella over his arm and 'The
Times' tucked under his other arm. Then a little old lady
with a battered old hat on, a bag full of shopping and fluffy
white hair. Behind her, a bedraggled me with scruffy jeans,
one bleeding knee, messed up hair and goofy teeth. Altogether
the worst one in that normal queue waiting for a normal bus
on that normal day in November.*

Lindsay Iles,
10 yrs.

●   **WHEN I'M OLD**

– –

This idea developed from the poem *'Warning'* by Jenny
Joseph in which she lists all of the things she would like to
feel free to do but can't because of the restraints of
convention. We all suffer from the 'what would the
neighbours think' attitude.

We suggest that you begin by asking the children to air their
grievances, the petty constraints that annoy them, – adults
pushing in front of them in shops or queues, being shushed
in libraries, rules of the home etc. Then after a good session
of moaning, read the Jenny Joseph poem and ask for comments.

Suggest then, that the class write a similar piece listing the
things they'd like to do but can't because they're children.

How do you end the piece? Do you encourage a defiant pose,
as with Ainne's example, or the realization that however
much you'd like things to be different, they never will be?

My favourite line was from a twelve year old lad who showed
no interest in the lesson except to chip in with –

> *"When I'm old I shall run through Harrods
> shouting 'Woolworths, Woolworths'."*

Warning

When I am an old woman I shall wear purple
With a red hat which doesn't go, and doesn't suit me.
And I shall spend my pension on brandy and summer gloves
And satin sandals, and say we've no money for butter.
I shall sit down on the pavement when I'm tired
And gobble up samples in shops and press alarm bells
And run my stick along the public railings
And make up for the sobriety of my youth.
I shall go out in my slippers in the rain
And pick flowers in other people's gardens
And learn to spit.

You can wear terrible shirts and grow more fat
And eat three pounds of sausages at a go
Or only bread and pickle for a week
And hoard pens and pencils and beermats and things in boxes.

But now me must have clothes that keep us dry
And pay our rent and not swear in the street
And set a good example for the children
We will have friends to dinner and read the papers.
But maybe I ought to practise a little now?
So people who know me are not too shocked and surprised
When suddenly I am old and start to wear purple.

Jenny Joseph

When I Am Old

When I am old I shall jump queues and push
    in front of children.
I shall let off stink-bombs in first-class
    hotels,
And I shall wear glasses like Elton John.
When I am an old woman I shall buy a parrot
    and teach it to swear.

But I am still a young girl,
So I must wait in queues,
Act polite in first-class hotels,
Not decorate my eyes
And I must not teach my parrot to swear.

Karla Grayling, 11 yrs.

When I'm Old

When I'm old I shall wrinkle up carpets
and leave them there,

and in shops I shall spend all my money
on cigarettes and chocolate.
I shall drink coffee all day
And have baked beans on Sundays.
When I'm old I shall giggle
and make a noise in libraries,
and pull out books and throw them on the floor.
I shall dye my hair blue and green
like Mollie Sugden
and not bother to brush my teeth
in the morning.
I shan't obey rules,
I shall throw bricks,
I'll be a stowaway on boats
and go round the world
and say 'fiddlesticks' to everyone!

Ainne Dennison, 11 yrs.

When I Am Old . . .

When I am old I will walk along the road
wearing multi-coloured stockings
with floppy garters matching,
and a straw hat with
buttercups and daisies.
When I am old I will go
to the flashy discos and dance till 2 o'clock
and NOT go to the granny mornings every Tuesday.
When I am old I will make twenty-one buns
with icing and plump cherries on top all for me!
(But what would the dentist say?)
But I'm only eleven
and it's a century to go before I'm old.

Hanora Hayes, 11 yrs.

●   **MIRRORS**

Begin by listing the many kinds of mirrors that we may glance
into during the course of a day – looking-glasses, shop
windows, reflections from water, eyes etc. Think too, of
mirrors in stories and legend – the wicked Queen in 'Snow
White', 'Alice through the Looking-Glass'.

Discussion begins in the concrete and then goes deeper into illusions, ambiguities etc. Can the mirror lie? Can we hide from mirrors? Does a mirror reflect back or swallow up an image? Does anyone like looking at the truth?

Try thinking of a mirror that could reflect the past or the future. The poem *'Mirror'* by Sylvia Plath is an excellent example to discuss.

● ### *Mirror*

I am silver and exact. I have no preconceptions.
Whatever I see I swallow immediately
Just as it is, unmisted by love or dislike.
I am not cruel, only truthful –
The eye of a little god, four-cornered.
Most of the time I meditate on the opposite wall.
It is pink, with speckles. I have looked at it so long
I think it is a part of my heart. But it flickers.
Faces and darkness separate us over and over.

Now I am a lake. A woman bends over me,
Searching my reaches for what she really is.
Then she turns to those liars, the candles or the moon.
I see her back, and reflect it faithfully.
She rewards me with tears and an agitation of hands
I am important to her. She comes and goes.
Each morning it is her face that replaces the darkness.
In me she has drowned a young girl, and in me an old woman
Rises towards her day after day, like a terrible fish.

● ### Mirrors

I can see you gazing out at me,
How I hate you.
Your boring eyes, your stubby nose,
Your goofy teeth and tattered clothes.
Just leave my world alone,
I don't need you.
With your snide remarks, unbrushed hair,
And your dirty looks, you just don't care.
What good are you anyway,
Is there anything you can do?
You've got no brains, you can't be jolly
You study hard, in childish folly.
Well I've got a way of leaving you,
leaving you way behind.
Take a brick and as you pass
Throw it hard, you'll smash the glass.   Katy Corlett,
I don't want mirrors.   14 yrs.

● *The Mirror*

I am cruel and cold,
Telling no lies just the truth.
I feel lonely and unwanted,
My glittering silver rim,
My clear and bare body.
Then over slithers the shadow
Wanting to know the truth.
I can't help myself,
I let the truth float out
And of course I get the blame.
Suddenly I become a target
For ornaments to be thrown at,
I become cut then shattered,
Will I ever be myself again?

Tracy Dee, 11 yrs.

● **WHEN I BLOW MY OWN TRUMPET**

– –

All children love to boast, to tell others of their skills, to impress. Here is a chance for children to really exaggerate their powers.

A discussion of the phrase 'blowing your own trumpet' can launch this idea and examples sought.

Then think of all the outrageous repercussions if trumpets were blown too loudly or for too long.

● *When I blow my own trumpet*

When I blow my own trumpet
people sigh behind cupped hands
and the curtains start to shake and tremble.

When I blow my own trumpet
the teacher reaches for her earphones
and the windows rattle with laughter.

When I blow my own trumpet
my buttons pop off
and my mouth bursts with lies.

When I blow my own trumpet
people turn and walk away
while my cat gives me a supercilious stare.

When I blow my own trumpet
the chairs hide under the table
and cups and saucers crack.

When I blow my own trumpet
my sister screams
and I shatter the T. V. screen.

Group Poem

●   **LUCKY/UNLUCKY**

Most children will quickly latch on to this exercise.

We all know people who we feel are luckier than us.

List a whole range of reasons for someone's good fortune,
and make them amusing where possible.

e.g.   *He was so lucky that he found a pearl in his*
                 boiled egg.

Conversely, make a list of reasons for someone's misfortune.

He was so unlucky
that his wig went bald
and the razor he bought went blunt.

He was so unlucky
that his dentist was an ex-builder.

He was so unlucky
that when he was a child he walked under a ladder
     thirteen times
and the decorators who decorated his house
     put wallpaper on the outside.

He was so unlucky
that his younger brother started playing the violin
     and his sister the cello.

Richard Webb, 11 yrs.

- -

Like all great races this demands silent concentration. The
teacher starts each two minute bout by telling the class the
title of the poem. They then have two minutes in which to
write down a short, precise piece. They should concentrate
on jotting down any words and ideas that leap into the mind.
The game borders on word association but can produce
surprising results. Good subjects include – moon, sun, stars,
night, dark, shadows, space, rocks, mirrors, windows, fire,
ice, snow, ponds, sea, rain, colours, feelings, seasons,
animals ... and even odd words such as 'cracked'. For a final
poem let the class each choose their own title.

The examples are from one session with a third year class:

●   *Night*

As black as blindness.
It creeps over villages.
Spreading the bright stars.

Debbie Osman,
10 yrs.

Cracked

    A broken egg.
The white spills out slowly seething
    over the polished table.

Debbie Osman, 10 yrs.

●   *Cracked*

As cracked as an old wall
As cracked as a fragile egg shell
As cracked as a piece of split wood
As cracked as a half shattered window
As cracked as time-worn, ancient manuscript
As cracked as Simon

Steven Wood, 10 yrs.

●   Space

The quiet bare moon
drifting through the freckled universe.
Craters grow like the human body.
Particles of rusty iron drift past the planet.
They are bleak and blind.

Simon Overbury, 9 yrs.

● **Bark**

Delicate fragments of tree-skin, minute details seen only
when fascinated by the marvels of it. Grooved like wrinkled flesh.

Steven Wood, 10 yrs.

Stones

Heated by the sun, cooled by wind, statues of themselves.
Beings that can't move from the inside. Observers of time.

Steven Wood

● ***Stone***

Cold, hard rock
Not at all like a baby's soft gentle skin.
Freckly surfaces.
Dull colours.
Heavy to lift.

Claire Baldwin, 9 yrs.

● **Dying**

A black death, slow, evil,
whispering in your ear:
"Its time to come with us"
Up to heaven.

Claire Baldwin, 9 yrs.

Window

Transparent,
a detective's eye,
sly and sleek,
peering into the open world.
Fragile,
it balances.

Simon Overbury, 9 yrs.

Towards the end of the session each child could take his or
her favourite idea and develop it further.

One

I may be
I may be small but I killed Goliath.
I may be silent but my thoughts tumble in like elephants.
I may be afraid but I've sailed rough seas in a wooden canoe.
I may be happy, sad, humble, big, fat, gentle etc.

Two

Wrestling
Either video a Saturday afternoon wrestling bout or talk about it with the class. Many children will have been to a live match. Try to capture the language of wrestling – names of falls, submissions etc. Try to build up a word picture of the atmosphere in the hall. How do the spectators react?

Three

Wrestling *(part two)*
How else do we wrestle?
I wrestled with my conscience . . .
with a problem . . .
with dreams, time, etc.

Four

Out of
Out of the horse's gallop his spirit tumbles.
Out of the summer flowers happy faces laugh
. . . etc.

Five

Sweet/Fruit poem
Each child brings in a sweet or a piece of fruit and examines it carefully. Look at it, touch it, smell it and finally taste it.
Soft centres, sherbert lemons, and Rolos etc are good sweets for this kind of writing.
Finally write up the finished piece on top of a colourful illustration of the sweet or fruit.

Six

Poetry is
Try to work out some new definitions of poetry.
Poetry is . . . the first spark of electricity from a
power station.

- *Poetry is ... a sweet smelling rose piercing a hand with its dagger like thorns.*
- *... the last lonely dinosaur looking for its lost companions.*

Seven
- **My horse**
  Describing an animal, perhaps a pet, in a mystical way, giving it supernatural qualities.
- *My horse is of the herd of fire, his eyes of amber wildly proud. His hooves are pure unbeaten gold, ... etc.*

Eight
- **It was so quiet**
  *It was so quiet
  that I could hear my thoughts snoring.
  It was so peaceful
  that I could hear a spider spinning its fragile web.*
- *It was so hushed, silent, etc.*

Nine
- **The empty classroom**
  Either after school or in the holidays.
- *Chairs stand alone on tables,
  their feet among the dust.
  Footsteps muddy and faded march
  around the floor.*

Ten
- **The gravestone**
  Visit a churchyard and from the details on a gravestone make up a poem.
- *Mary Oxley, widow of David Oxley,
  lies herself dead.
  An engraved cross at the top,
  a block of stone, six feet of earth, a coffin and
  then her,
  lying silently, sleeping till eternity.
  Grass shooting up, the beginnings of a tree.
  Died at Chiddingly
  March 12th 1881, aged 86 years.*

FURTHER BOOKS WHICH MAY PROVE USEFUL:

Does it Have to Rhyme and *What Rhymes with SECRET?* both by Sandy Brownjohn, published by Hodder & Stoughton, 1980 & 1982.

Imaginative Speech and Writing by Ronald James and R.G. Gregory, published by Nelson.

English Through Poetry Writing by Brian Powell – Heinemann Educational Publications.

Wishes, Lies and Dreams and *Rose, Where did you get that Red?* both by Kenneth Koch and published by Perennial Library, Harper and Row. (These are American books that may be ordered through British bookshops.)

Children as Writers – Award winning entries from the W.H. Smith Young Writers Competition. Published annually by Heinemann.

Poets in Schools Edited by Alisdair Aston and published by Harrap.

Creative writing for Juniors by Barry Maybury, published by Batsford.

How to write by John Fairfax and John Moat, published by Elm Tree Books.

Writers' Workshop by Barry Maybury, published by Batsford.

Poetry in the Making by Ted Hughes, published by Faber.

Encouraging Writing by Robert Protherough, and *Poetry Experience* by Stephen Tunnicliffe, both published by Methuen.

Schools Poetry Association, magazines, anthologies and broadsheets available from S.P.A., Twyford School, Winchester, Hants.

Becoming a Writer – a course for teachers involved with developing Infants' writing, available from Kent County Council, County Hall, Maidstone, Kent.

● **RECOMMENDED ANTHOLOGIES AND INDIVIDUAL COLLECTIONS OF POETRY:**

– –

The Oxford Poetry Books Nos. 1–5. compiled by John Foster, (OUP)
Delights and Warnings Ed. John and Gillian Beer (Macdonald)
Strictly Private Ed. by Roger McGough (Kestrel & Puffin)
I Like this Poem Ed. Kaye Webb (Puffin)
Soundings Ed. Kit Wright (Heinemann Educational)
Rabbiting On and *Hot Dog* both by Kit Wright (Fontana Lions and Puffin)
Salford Road – Gareth Owen (Kestrel)
Mind Your Own Business – Michael Rosen (Fontana Lions)
Tower Blocks (Poems of the City) – Marion Lines (Franklin Watts)
In the Glassroom – Roger McGough (Cape)
You Tell Me – Roger McGough and Michael Rosen (Puffin)
Penguin Modern European Poets, particularly Miroslav Holub.
Chatto Poets for the Young, particularly Brian Jones *The Spitfire on the Northern Line.*

ACKNOWLEDGEMENTS

We are indebted to those teaching colleagues who helped us develop our approach, and to the children we have taught whose ideas have often been far better than our own. Furthermore we would like to acknowledge the support of our headmasters, in particular Graham Bond, who encouraged us to prepare this manual for use in school, and that of Roy Calthorpe, Art Adviser for East Sussex, who encouraged us to share our ideas at Teachers' Centres. Also we should mention the support of the Education Secretaries at the National Poetry Society – Pat Swell and Michelle Fink, the South East Arts Literature Officer, John Rice, and the General Inspector for English in Surrey, D. Eccles, all of whom gave us opportunities to try out our ideas in Public, Comprehensive, Middle and Junior Schools.

Work by Children

Our thanks to the following schools for permission to reprint work by children: Marshlands C.P. School, Hailsham; King Offa C.J. School, Bexhill; Freda Gardham C.P. School, Rye; Lynsted School, Nr. Sittingbourne; Willingdon Comprehensive, Eastbourne; Hailsham School; Plumpton C.P. School, Lewes; Durrington High School, Hove; Tunbury C.P. School, Walderslade, Chatham.

Some of the poems reproduced appeared in Marshlands School Magazines, school poetry anthologies – 'Fire-lit Eyes', 'Caught in the Spotlight', 'Words out of our World', 'Glass Menagerie', and 'Poets in Schools' publications from Durrington High School and Plumpton C.P. School. 'Body Sounds' by Katya Haine was televised by the BBC in 1979, 'Angel Faces' by Debbie Osman in 1980, and 'When I'm Old' by Karla Grayling by both BBC and ITV in 1980. 'Angel Faces' and 'When I'm Old' were placed first and second respectively in the National Poetry Society's Young Poets Competition in 1980 and subsequently printed in *South East Arts Review* (Autumn 1980).

The following won prizes in the W.H. Smith Young Writers' Competition and were printed in *Children as Writers* for the appropriate year: 'The Sun Rise' by Amanda Cornwell, 'There is a Pig' by Emavel Rodriguez and 'My Hand' by Mark Sheppard (1983), 'This Morning' and 'He Is' by Tim Clapham (1982), 'Whose Angel Are You?' by John Flann (1981), 'Body Sounds' by Katya Haine and 'Colours' by Judy-Jane McGuire (1980), 'Fox' and 'What You Are' by Hayley Kemp, and 'To be alone' by Matthew Cole (1979).

'Tonight at Noon' by Barry Harvey was printed in *Martlet* – an anthology of writing by young people in East Sussex.

'The Dragons Inside Me' and 'Gargoyle' by Lindsay Iles, and 'Six ways of looking at a Pond' by Kathryn Hoblin were printed in *'Identity Parade'* (a South East Arts anthology of writing by young people in Kent, Surrey and East Sussex). 'The Dragons Inside Me' also received a prize in the Downland Poets Competition 1980.

'In the 13th Hour' by Tim Clapham appeared in *A4* published by the Schools Poetry Association 1983.

'Tonight at Noon' by Barry Harvey, 'Bus Queue' by Lindsay Iles, and 'When I'm Old' by Anne Dennison, all appeared in *Northern Line* – a quarterly magazine of work by young writers.

Wherever possible we have credited the original sources of any ideas that are not of our own devising. In some cases, the origins and inspiration behind an idea may have been 'lost in the mists of time' and anyone who feels that credit is due should contact the publishers so that they may be acknowledged in future editions.

Poems included in the text: 'Wilderness' by Carl Sandburg from *Corn Huskers* (Harcourt, Brace, Jovanovich Inc.); 'Tonight at Noon' by Adrian Henri and 'What You Are' by Roger McGough from *Penguin Modern Poets 10 – The Mersey Sound (1967)*; 'A Boy's Head' by Miroslav Holub from *Selected Poems*, trans. Ina Milner and George Theiner, *Penguin Modern European Poets, (1967)*; 'Mirror' by Sylvia Plath from *Crossing the Water* (Faber); 'Warning' by Jenny Joseph from *New Poems* (1963). 'Heron' by Edwin Morgan from *Glasgow to Saturn*, Carcanet. 'Hyena' by Edwin Morgan.

Poems referred to in the text may be found in the following sources: '14 Ways of Touching Peter' by George MacBeth – *The Book of Cats* Ed. by George MacBeth and Martin Booth (Penguin 1979); 'I Want to Paint' by Adrian Henri – *Penguin Modern Poets 10 – The Mersey Sound*; 'A Small Dragon' by Brian Patten – *Penguin Modern Poets 10*. Further examples of haikus and tankas may be found in *The Penguin Book of Japanese Verse* trans. Geoffrey Bownas and Anthony Thwaite (Penguin 1964).

The song 'Clown' by Ralph McTell may be found on *The Ralph McTell Collection* (Pickwick Records) or *Ralph McTell Re-visited* (Transatlantic Records).

The editor and publisher wish to thank the following for permission to reprint copyright poems in this anthology:
Adrian Henri: 'Tonight at Noon' from *Penguin Modern Poets 10 – The Mersey Sound* (Penguin Books, 1967), © Adrian Henri 1967. Miroslav Holub: 'A Boy's Head' from *Selected Poems – Penguin Modern European Poets* (Penguin Books, 1967), © Miroslav Holub 1967, Translation copyright © Penguin Books, 1967. Jenny Joseph: 'Warning' from *Rose in the Afternoon* (J.M. Dent, 1974), © Jenny Joseph 1985. Roger McGough: 'What You Are' from *Penguin Modern Poets 10 – The Mersey Sound* (Penguin Books, 1967), © Roger McGough 1967. Edwin Morgan: 'Heron'; 'Hyena', © Edwin Morgan 1985. Sylvia Plath: 'Mirror' from *Crossing the Water* (Faber), © Ted Hughes, 1971, by permission of Olwyn Hughes. Carl Sandburg: 'Wilderness' from *Cornhuskers*, © 1918 by Holt, Rinehart and Winston, Inc., renewed 1946 by Carl Sandburg. Reprinted by permission of Harcourt, Brace, Jovanovitch Inc. 1985.